HOW TO CHOOSE THE RIGHT PERSON FOR THE RIGHT JOB EVERY TIME

LORI DAVILA
LOUISE KURSMARK

McGraw-Hill

New York   Chicago   San Francisco   Lisbon   London
Madrid   Mexico City   Milan   New Delhi
San Juan   Seoul   Singapore
Sydney   Toronto

The McGraw·Hill Companies

4 5 6 7 8 9 0 DOC/DOC 0 9 8 7 6

ISBN 0-07-143123-3

This publication is designed to provide accurate and authoritative information in regard to the subject matter covered. It is sold with the understanding that the publisher is not engaged in rendering legal, accounting, or other professional service. If legal advice or other expert assistance is required, the services of a competent professional person should be sought.

—From a declaration of principles jointly adopted by a committee of the American Bar Association and a committee of publishers.

McGraw-Hill books are available at special quantity discounts to use as premiums and sales promotions, or for use in corporate training programs. For more information, please write to the Director of Special Sales, Professional Publishing, McGraw-Hill, Two Penn Plaza, New York, NY 10121-2298. Or contact your local bookstore.

Library of Congress Cataloging-in-Publication Data

Davila, Lori.
  How to choose the right person for the right job every time /
Lori Davila and Louise Kursmark.
    p. cm.
  Includes index.
  ISBN 0-07-143123-3 (alk. paper)
    1. Employment interviewing. 2. Employee selection.
I. Kursmark, Louise. II. Title.
  HF5549.5.I6D38 2004
  658.3'1124—dc22

                                        2004009354

Contents

Acknowledgments

This book is dedicated to our nieces, nephews, and children:
Greg Finestine, Jennifer Finestine, Robert Craig,
Lauren Craig, Jennifer Anderson, Meredith Kursmark,
and Matt Kursmark. May you find fulfillment, success, and passion
as you embark on your careers, and may you make a difference in
the world with your unique gifts.

THIS BOOK COULD NOT have been conceived or written without the help of so many wonderful people. I'd like especially to thank Kris Maher of the *Wall Street Journal*; my delightful and knowledgeable editor, Donya Dickerson, and all the wonderful behind-the-scenes people at McGraw-Hill; my talented coauthor, Louise, for taking on this project with me; Norm Mitchell for giving me a chance; Diana Bragg for believing in me; and all the wonderful clients and business associates who have recently come into my life. A big thank you goes to my parents, Sam and Harriet Gitow, for your love, support, wisdom, and courage, and to Wendy, Billy, and the rest of my extended family for always being there. Last but not least, this book would not have been possible without the support of my husband, Mike—my best friend, my soul mate, and my life's partner. I've learned from all of you to reach for the stars and to believe.

—Lori Davila

Every new project brings delightful new connections and interesting new challenges. I am eternally grateful to Lori for inviting me to join her on this book and for being so understanding of my work style and schedule. Working with Donya and all of the folks at McGraw-Hill has been pleasurable and stress-free. I am grateful to my terrific clients and my executive networking group for providing context and the opportunity to test theories in the real world. And my husband, Bob, has as always been an anchor, stay, and support who makes it possible for me to continue an exciting professional journey.

—Louise Kursmark

We are also grateful to the following individuals and organizations for their assistance:

Society for Human Resource Management (SHRM); The Society for Industrial and Organizational Psychology (SIOP); *HR Magazine*; *HR Executive*; William C. Byham of DDI; Michael Foster of AIRS; Alice Snell of iLogos Research; Tim Vigue of Novations Group, Inc.; Heather Hartmann of Staffing.org; Dr. John Sullivan; Cathy Fyock; Dr. Richard Harding of Kenexa; Bill Anstine of Kenexa; Peter Vogt; Walt Gansser; Laura May; Clemist Jackson; Peter Weddle; Anne Griffin of Kennedy Information; Eileen Woods; Linda Bodner; Joe Houde; Gail Auerbach; Joanne DeLavan Reichardt; Dean Madison; Jeff Hall; Gary Cluff; Tom Ruby; Lance Trenary; Judy Irwin; Janet Taylor; Sam Rotella; Chuck Russell; Mark Brenner; Tim Moran; Kathy O'Connell, Paul Lutmer, and Cheryl Brantmeier; and Paul Bowen and Judy Mebane.

Introduction

IF YOU ARE LIKE MOST MANAGERS, human resources professionals, and business owners, you frequently have a difficult time hiring the right employees for your organization. You may be gun-shy because several previous new hires have not worked out and you are left with mediocre and poor performers. You are expected to hire top performers who are the right fit for your company while exposing job candidates' liabilities before it's too late. You don't have hiring processes in place, you haven't been formally trained in interviewing skills, and you're uncomfortable with making one more hiring decision.

The most important aspect of hiring top performers is asking the right interview questions and properly evaluating the data gathered during interviews. Yet the interview process can leave you with more questions than answers if you're not prepared and if you don't know what to ask.

How This Book Can Help You

This book is designed as an easy-to-use guide for people who are already busy with their day-to-day duties and who need immediate results. You will learn how to make your hiring decisions with complete confidence by using a proven, step-by-step interviewing system. To choose the right employee, it is critical to identify not just technical skills but also behaviors, motivations, and the type of environment in which the employee will excel. In this book you will find 401 interview questions and 50 competency areas and "job-fit" motivator categories. You can simply choose questions from the most important categories, or you can design your own questions using the techniques outlined. You will learn how to draw out the candidate information that you need to make a proper evaluation.

How the Book Is Organized

Chapter 1 makes a case for making a change. The costs of hiring the wrong employee are high, and this chapter delineates those costs and shows a direct link between sound hiring choices and financial returns. If you are already convinced, you can use the information in this chapter to build support for a change within your organization. An exercise will help you rate the current status of your hiring activities.

Chapter 2 introduces Behavior-Based Interviewing—the strategy we recommend for choosing the right person for the right job every time. You will learn a bit about the history of the concept and its proven benefits, such as greater productivity, reduced turnover, increased employee job satisfaction and morale, and enhanced diversity. You will be able to compare Behavior-Based Interview questions with the traditional and situational questions that are commonly used in companies of all types, and after you've finished the chapter, you can test your knowledge of these three types of interview questions.

In Chapter 3 you will find a five-step process for conducting Behavior-Based Interviews. Ample examples are included to connect the concepts to real-world applications in companies like yours. This chapter will ingrain the practice of Behavior-Based Interviewing—you will understand how to identify core competency areas and success factors, select appropriate questions, conduct a successful interview, and evaluate candidates' responses using an easy system that rates evidence, not impressions.

If you have someone coming in for an interview tomorrow, skip immediately to Chapter 4—it contains 401 interview questions and can serve as your instant and ongoing resource for choosing the right questions for every new hire and promotion at your company. This chapter also contains icebreaking questions, follow-up questions, and traditional and situational questions with which you can round out your interview sessions. But be sure to go back afterwards and read the remaining chapters to polish your interview skills.

Chapter 5 shares six success stories from companies that use Behavior-Based Interviewing as a core business practice. From TD Madison and Associates, with fewer than 10 employees, to 300,000-employee GE, these companies share a deep commitment to the practice and have reaped significant benefits from its companywide implementation.

Chapter 6 contains an overview of legal interview questions and hiring practices. Behavior-Based Interviewing is inherently fair and entirely legal because it asks candidates about their past performance, not about perceived limitations or factors that are irrelevant to the job. But you will want to review this chapter to be sure that your company is remaining within legal guidelines in all of its interview questions and at every step of the interview and selection process.

In Chapter 7 we share information on how candidates prepare for interviews and give you some guidance for getting the best answers to your interview questions, regardless of the candidate's level of preparation. We've provided several scenarios, along with "Interviewer's Tips" that will help you overcome roadblocks that stand in the way of getting complete and accurate responses from diverse candidates.

The process of implementing a Behavior-Based Interviewing program at your company is discussed in Chapter 8. Each step is described in detail; we have also identified potential "showstoppers" along the way—obstacles or situations that could derail your program—and we give advice and suggestions for getting over, around, or through these obstacles.

In Chapter 9 we give you a step-by-step guide for evaluating your Behavior-Based Interviewing process on an ongoing basis and discuss other elements of your hiring process, such as résumé assessment, telephone screening, testing and assessments, and reference checking.

And finally, we include two appendices, the first an extensive resource list of organizations that can help you implement a Behavior-Based Interviewing program at your company, and the second a selection of forms. Within the chapters we discuss the forms extensively and show you filled-in examples, and in the appendix we provide the blank forms so that you can copy them and use them for your own program.

By following this book's guidelines, you can build an organization of top performers that you can be proud of. With the right people in place, your company can compete effectively by delivering cutting-edge products and services, and it can react quickly to market demands. Other results might include a boost in your company's revenues, service levels, and reputation. The right-fit employee will increase productivity and employee morale, and he or she will adjust faster, reducing training time and costs. Your employee turnover rate will decrease dramatically, and you will build a highly skilled organization.

It all starts with hiring the right employees, and this book will give you the understanding and the easy-to-implement, practical tools to create a hiring process that delivers proven results, time after time.

Your Hiring Decisions Will Either Make or Break Your Company

The kind of people I look for to fill top management spots are the eager beavers, the mavericks. These are the guys who try to do more than they're expected to do—they always reach.

—Lee Iacocca

I F IT FEELS TO YOU LIKE we've been on a business roller coaster lately, your feeling is absolutely right. We've seen it all in recent times—the boom, the bust, the burn, and a very slow recovery. We enjoyed several years of extraordinary economic growth and record-breaking corporate earnings. Who could have forecasted what followed? The collapse of dot-com companies, the horrific events of September 11, a major nosedive in the stock market, a recession, high-profile corporate corruption, a war, and, at the time this book is being written, an unemployment rate above 6 percent. Yet it is predicted that in the coming years there will again be a tremendous shortage of workers because 40 percent of the workforce is headed toward retirement.

Companies today are coping with an unprecedented volume of applicants for their open positions. Job seekers are sending out three to four times the number of résumés that they used to, and because of the Internet, they can apply for job opportunities easily and often—24 hours a day. Several years ago you were lucky to get a handful of responses to your job advertisements; today you might get hundreds and even thousands of responses. The volume of applicants won't go away even when the economy turns around. It may be easier to find people, but it's getting more and more challenging to find the *right* people.

The good news in this challenging scenario is that companies are refocusing on the quality of their hires. During the boom, the trend was to hire people fast and furiously. Employment experts called this phenomenon the "warm-body syndrome." But as companies have downsized and cut their workforces to the absolute bare minimum, it has become even more imperative to bring in the best talent when hiring for future openings. Companies are beginning to recognize that they can't settle for less than high-end producers, and the days of offering jobs to marginal candidates, a practice that characterized the boom era, are long gone. There are only so many seats and so many hours in the day, and those seats and hours must be maximized to the fullest extent possible.

As we move forward with recovery, it's becoming even more important to analyze the fit of a candidate up front—you can't throw darts anymore. You want to be certain that you select employees who will match the job requirements most closely while fitting in with your company's culture and team members. After all, performance in the workplace doesn't just depend on specific job skills. People must be motivated to perform well, and what motivates one person might be very different from what motivates another. To be sure of hiring right-fit candidates, then, the hiring process must include ways to identify the motivators and environmental factors that will prompt an employee's best effort. It *can* be done—this book teaches you how.

The Bottom Line

The new economy is recognized as the knowledge economy. Wall Street now acknowledges that a significant component of a company's value lies in the brainpower of its employees, not just in the company's tangible assets. The major outcome of this principle is an emphasis on top-quality employees who have the capability to increase company value. And so the business case is building that there is a direct link between sound hiring choices and a company's financial returns.

Several studies prove this linkage, including Watson Wyatt's Human Capital Index. This study, conducted in 1999 and repeated in 2001, measures several dimensions of "human capital excellence" to determine whether good practices have any effect on a company's bottom line. Indeed they do. High scores on the Human Capital Index are clearly correlated with greater market value. In other words, the better an organization is doing in managing its human capital, the better its returns to shareholders. Most relevant to our topic, one of the practices measured in this study is "recruiting and retention excellence." This factor alone is associated with a 7.9 percent increase in market value. These data provide compelling evidence that hiring talented employees results in improved company performance. After all, it is the talented leaders, line managers, and employees who implement the strategies and deliver the competitive products to the marketplace.

Successful business leaders agree that their most valuable asset is their people and that best-fit employees are key to a company's future success. If the wrong people are manufacturing, selling, and servicing a product, no matter how great the company, its performance will automatically decline.

Hiring as a Top Strategic Business Priority

More and more business leaders are mandating that all business decisions made throughout their organizations create value, beginning with making the right hiring decisions. This is a critical step in producing leading-edge performance, and all hiring managers must be held accountable for these decisions. Shareholders benefit from companies that focus on implementing sound hiring practices and that make smart hiring a top strategic business priority. Hiring the right people and creating an organization that instills innovation and increases profits will allow employees, customers, and shareholders all to reap the rewards.

Hiring Mistakes Are Costly

When you develop a sound hiring and interviewing process, you will begin to hire employees who bring value to your organization. These new employees will earn you money rather than cost you money. If you still need convincing, calculate the cost of just one hiring mistake. Once you understand the economic impact on your business, you should be ready to take the necessary steps to get the process back on track.

Table 1-1
Cost of a Bad Hire

POSITION TITLE _____

Step 1. Check all the items listed below that apply.

Step 2. Calculate the cost of each item checked.

Step 3. Total all the costs to determine the cost of a bad hire.

RECRUITING COSTS

❑ Advertising $_____

❑ Recruiters (hours spent × hourly rate) $_____

❑ Administrator (hours spent × hourly rate) $_____

❑ Candidate travel costs (airfare, hotel, meals, meeting space) $_____

❑ Interviews (interviewer's time spent × rate) $_____

❑ Background checks and investigations $_____

❑ Other $_____

SALARY AND BENEFITS COSTS

❑ Monthly salary × number of months employed $_____

❑ Estimated benefits (often calculated as 35% of salary) $_____

❑ Signing bonus $_____

OTHER SIGNIFICANT COSTS

❑ Training and orientation (trainer, manager, and other employees' time spent × rate) $_____

❑ Training materials $_____

❑ Relocation costs $_____

❑ New employee setup costs (computer, phone, tools) $_____

❑ Litigation costs, if applicable $_____

❑ Other $_____

TOTAL COST OF A BAD HIRE $_____

Next, look around you and ask yourself how many hiring mistakes you already have in your organization. Can you afford to make one more mistake by leaving your next hiring decision to chance? The costs and the stakes are too high, and such a mistake can threaten your company's overall performance.

A widely quoted study by Harvard University indicates that 80 percent of employee turnover is due to hiring mistakes. And hiring mistakes are costly—from one and a half times the annual salary for an entry-level employee to over ten times the annual salary for a senior-level executive. At an annual wage rate of $50,000, turnover can cost a company well over $75,000 for each departing employee. The higher the salary, the higher the cost, as higher-paid employees have a greater impact on operations and business relationships. And the cost can escalate the longer it takes to solve the problem.

The Real Cost of Hiring the Wrong Person

The cost of making a hiring mistake can be easily measured. The worksheet in Table 1-1 will help you calculate the cost of a single hiring mistake.

Hidden Costs

In addition to these obvious costs, you should also consider the hidden costs, such as lost productivity, missed opportunities, dissatisfied customers, damage to project continuity, lowered employee morale, and loss of a competitive edge. Lost productivity is easy to measure in manufacturing—for example, a top performer may be turning out 80 widgets an hour and a poor performer may be turning out only an unacceptable 15 widgets per hour. Lost opportunities in sales revenue may be calculated by subtracting the revenue generated by your bad hire from the revenue generated by one of your top performers.

What may be difficult to quantify is how your bad hire may have damaged customer and employee relationships. What is the cost of just one lost customer or one delayed project? If your company develops a reputation for high turnover and low employee morale, attracting top-performing candidates will become even more difficult. Managers may be more focused on continuously filling open positions than on more important strategic and team-building initiatives.

It's not enough just to know the cost factors. Your organization must act in ways that will improve its bottom line, and the costs of a bad hiring decision can be debilitating to any business. And because hiring is a complex process, there are many opportunities for that bad decision to be made—and made again and again. To avoid making and repeating mistakes, you must identify and root out the causes of bad hiring at your company. Then you must create a process that empowers and enables you to hire the right person for the right job, every time. This book tells you how.

Top 10 Hiring Mistakes

Whether your company is large or small, whether you're hiring an entry-level employee or a top executive, any one of the following mistakes can result in a hiring disaster for your organization.

1. Not Knowing What You Are Looking For

If you're like most hiring managers, you haven't carefully thought out the specific skills, behaviors, characteristics, motivators, and competencies that will indicate that a person will be a top performer in your open position. If you don't have a job description, work with others who are familiar with the position to develop one that is accurate. A clear picture of the successful candidate is an important guide for hiring, especially if you are working with recruiters and other job applicant screeners. Identify what motivates your customers and what drives value for your company so that you can find the right people to deliver those things. The more clearly your requirements are spelled out, the better able you will be to assess how ideal a candidate really is. Invest the time up front and you will save countless hours, headaches, and dollars later on.

2. Inadequate Interview Preparation

Most hiring managers give little thought to the interview. Executive search firm TD Madison and Associates cites a recent survey of hiring managers that revealed that more than 70 percent of all managers spend less than 5 minutes preparing for interviews. Interviewers who don't plan ahead risk not getting the quality of information that is necessary to make a good hiring decision. Prepare your questions well in advance so that you don't end up having an irrelevant conversation with the candidate. The questions should be crafted to identify hidden liabilities and determine whether the candidate is a good fit for the job and the company. The inability to ask the right questions can lead to a misinterpretation of your discussion. Keep formal notes to accurately record what is said during interviews. Make sure your job requirements and performance expectations are clear. Hiring errors are often made because not enough information is gathered and improper assumptions are made. Take the interviewing process very seriously, because the success of your company and your career depends on it.

3. Poor Selection of Interview Questions

Questions should be well prepared in advance and should be developed to reveal a candidate's technical skills, knowledge, behaviors, likes, dislikes, and key motivators. It's not enough to know whether a candidate can do the job. It's equally important to know whether the person will fit your organization and whether the candidate will be motivated to do the job. Good managers ask probing questions to determine if the candidate is absolutely the right choice. Hypothetical questions are often asked during interviews. The problem with hypothetical questions is that they are not based upon past performance, but only on what the job candidate thinks is the right answer. Try to avoid closed questions that elicit one-word answers. Questions that begin with "tell me about," "describe," and "give me an example" will provide much more information. Proper preparation will also reduce the risk that you will ask illegal questions without realizing it and expose your organization to lawsuits.

4. Hiring Too Quickly

If your primary business responsibilities do not include hiring, you might be tempted to fill openings too quickly so that you can do your real job. This can make you susceptible to candidates who interview well but lack the critical skills needed to perform the job successfully. You may place too much emphasis on a candidate's experience rather than on the candidate's ability to do the job. Hiring quickly relieves impatient hiring managers and overwhelmed team members, but in their haste to relieve the business burden, many managers overlook signs of trouble and don't do their full due diligence.

5. No Awareness of the Halo Effect

The halo effect occurs when you like a candidate because you find that you have something in common with that person. Perhaps she is from your hometown, he attended the same college as you, or the two of you share a common interest. Suddenly that person can do no wrong, and you're sure the candidate will make a wonderful employee. Hiring is a lot like dating. Love at first sight can be blinding, especially when it comes to hiring the right person for the job. The halo effect can blind you to the candidate's liabilities.

6. Hiring People Just Like You

Most people tend to choose candidates whose style and viewpoints are similar to their own. Many managers believe that the key to hiring the best person for the job is to go with their gut and trust their intuition. Too many people react favorably to people whom they perceive to be just like themselves. However, this similarity does not necessarily mean that these candidates are suitable for certain jobs. Without practice, inexperienced managers can allow one positive characteristic to outshine the others. Don't let a good first impression unjustifiably influence you.

7. Raising Standards Unrealistically

Some managers are using the large volume of candidates as an opportunity to set unnecessarily high standards for open positions. Instead of requiring a bachelor's degree, they ask for an advanced degree or 5 to 10 years of additional experience. This approach leads to hiring people who are overqualified for the position and underchallenged by it, a definite setup for future problems.

8. Using Only One Interviewer

The decision to fill a position is too important to have it hinge on one person's contact with the candidate. Exposure to other interviewers could very well reveal aspects of the candidate that you might not have seen yourself. Sharing interview results and reaching a consensus can assist you in making an accurate hiring decision. Everyone involved in the interview process must be knowledgeable about interviewing techniques, including what questions they can and cannot ask. In addition, using more than one interviewer will keep job candidates on their toes.

9. No Interviewing Process in Place

Are you using a highly subjective approach to making your hiring decisions rather than a well-thought-out, structured, and proven hiring process? Given how important hiring top people is to a company's success, more attention and more resources must be invested to make hiring a formal business process. Most people in business today do not realize that interviewing a candidate is a technical skill. In the vast majority of today's interviews, it is the candidate who has prepared, rehearsed, practiced, and been coached. If you were able to implement a streamlined hiring process, if all managers in your company who conducted interviews were trained, and if you held your hiring initiatives in the highest regard, you would have an enormous competitive edge. The key to an interview's effectiveness is the method with which it is prepared and delivered. Give this top priority and you can dramatically improve the performance levels of your organization.

10. Not Checking References Thoroughly

If you are being held accountable for your hiring decisions, you need to do your own reference checks. It is a good idea to talk to others who know the candidate in addition to the references provided. With the candidate's permission, try former employers, recognizing the limits of such sources. Look for consistency between the interview and the references.

Exercise—Rate Your Hiring Efforts

Rate your own hiring efforts by reviewing these warning signs that may apply to you and your company. The presence of these business issues may not point exclusively to a problem with your hiring efforts, as other variables may be equally important. But if you answer no to more than three of the following questions, you should invest time in reviewing your hiring efforts.

Check either Yes or No.

Yes	No	
_____	_____	Is hiring a top company priority?
_____	_____	Does your company have a hiring strategy in place?

Yes	No	
_____	_____	Is your company considered an employer of choice?
_____	_____	Is your employee turnover rate decreasing?
_____	_____	Is employee morale improving?
_____	_____	Are your customer satisfaction scores improving?
_____	_____	Are your profit margins improving?
_____	_____	Is the number of lost business opportunities decreasing?
_____	_____	Are employee performance appraisal scores rising?
_____	_____	Are hiring expenses decreasing?
_____	_____	Is there a decrease in the number of incomplete projects?
_____	_____	Is employee productivity improving?
_____	_____	Is the quality of your products and services improving?
_____	_____	Are work teams becoming more stable and experienced?
_____	_____	Does your company have positive name recognition?

There's no doubt about it, good hiring must be a strategic priority for successful companies. Hiring mistakes cost your company money in both the short term (replacing poor performers) and the long term (dragging down market value).

The good news is that it is possible to ingrain good hiring practices within an organization. You can implement a system and create the processes to make good hiring "standard operating procedure" at your company. We believe that Behavior-Based Interviewing is the most reliable, predictable, and successful method to ensure good hires. In the next chapters, you'll learn more about Behavior-Based Interviewing, how it will transform your hiring practices, and the five easy steps to master the process and make it a reality within your organization.

Take the Guesswork Out of Hiring with Behavior-Based Interviewing

You give me the right people and I don't care what organization you give me. Good things will happen. Give me the wrong people, and it doesn't matter what you do with the organization. Bad things will happen.

—Colin Powell

THE JOB INTERVIEW is the tool that is relied on most in making employment decisions. Yet, as you read in Chapter 1, hiring managers frequently make mistakes by wrongly relying on gut feelings, by preparing poorly for interviews, and by asking interview questions that don't allow them to assess candidates accurately and identify their liabilities. So how do you scratch beneath the surface to determine whether a candidate really has what it takes to be a top performer? By finding out what that individual is capable of accomplishing in the workplace and by using an interview process designed for that precise purpose.

When you buy a new car, you take it for a test drive, look under the hood, and kick the tires to see how it will really perform on the road. When you shop for a new pair of shoes, you try them on to see how they fit before you buy them. Doesn't it make sense to have an interviewing process that allows you to test-drive a candidate before you buy? One where you can see how a candidate will respond in real-life situations and one that enables you to look under the hood to reveal the candidate's skills, motivations, and behaviors and to determine whether that candidate would be a good fit for your organization? Why struggle through one more interview without a process in place? Manufacturing has a process. Sales has a process. Your organization's hiring practices also need a structured process.

A highly effective interviewing process is available, and it can easily be implemented within your organization's current hiring practices. It's called Behavior-Based Interviewing, and it is rapidly becoming the preferred interviewing method for companies of all sizes and in all industries. No other interviewing method has proved as accurate in identifying performance effectiveness. In fact, a research study performed by the University of Waterloo in Ontario, Canada, revealed that conventional interviews lead to selection of the best candidate only 19 percent of the time. Organizations would be better off throwing dice or flipping a coin to make their hiring choices. According to that same study, Behavior-Based Interviewing techniques boost the success rate to 75 percent. A successfully implemented Behavior-Based Interviewing process allows hiring managers to predict, accurately and with confidence, a candidate's potential for success on the job.

An added advantage of Behavior-Based Interviewing is that it is, by its very nature, nondiscriminatory. Rather than focusing on *disabilities*, Behavior-Based Interviewing allows candidates to express their *abilities*. Preselected questions, carefully correlated with the essential functions of the job, allow candidates to describe specific examples of their past behavior. Careless questions are avoided, and the risk of straying into potentially biased questioning is sharply reduced.

The roots of Behavior-Based Interviewing date back to the 1970s, when industrial psychologists studying traditional interviews concluded that when used alone, these interviews weren't effective in accurately predicting a candidate's capability to perform a job. That is because traditional interview questions are often hypothetical or theoretical. Job candidates often respond with hypothetical answers that reflect what they think the interviewer wants to hear. Their answers don't accurately represent what they would do in real-life situations.

An example of a traditional question is, "What would you do if a team member wasn't contributing to a project you were working on?" A candidate would most likely respond with a hypothetical answer such as, "I would ask them if they fully understood the requirements of the project and if they needed my assistance." This answer doesn't provide solid evidence about the candidate's ability to lead and motivate others effectively.

An interviewer using behavior-based techniques could ask the same question this way: "Tell me about a specific time when a team member wasn't contributing to a project you were working on. What was the situation, and what steps did you take to resolve the problem? What was the outcome?" Behavior-Based Interview questions ask for specific examples of past experiences and are followed up with probing questions to get the information that is needed to make a sound hiring decision. The questions are meaningful and are aimed at getting factual, job-related answers. Much as a skilled journalist asks questions to get at the root of a story, you as the interviewer must have a specific line of questioning prepared to get the facts.

In a Behavior-Based Interview, you ask questions that usually begin with "Tell me about a time when . . ." or "Give me an example of when . . ." or "Describe a situation when . . . " The questions are open-ended and require much more than a yes or no response. Some examples of Behavior-Based questions are:

- "Tell me about a time when you had many projects due all at the same time."
- "Give me an example of when you came up with a cost-cutting idea."
- "Describe an innovate idea that you developed that led to the success of a company initiative."

As you can see, Behavior-Based Interview questions differ from traditional questions in that they demand detailed examples that illustrate how a candidate has performed a specific skill or demonstrated a particular competency. This kind of response allows interviewers to assess each candidate fairly and to base hiring decisions on proven capabilities, not glib talk or the image the candidate projects during an interview. As a result, employers can avoid the poor hiring statistics that result from traditional interviewing—remember, the rate of successful hires using traditional methods is just 19 percent, while with Behavior-Based Interviewing, it zooms to 75 percent!

Past Performance Is the Best Predictor of Future Success

The basic premise behind Behavior-Based Interviewing is that past performance is the best indicator of future success on the job. It is the best interviewing technique available today, as it allows you to thoroughly, fairly, and accurately assess candidates better than any other interviewing method. In a Behavior-Based Interview, your questions allow the candidate to demonstrate his or her competencies by providing specific and detailed examples from past work experiences. This way, the candidate can't simply talk about what he or she "might" or "would" do in a given hypothetical situation.

Behavior in this usage is defined as a candidate's past performance, specific experiences, and measurable accomplishments. In Behavior-Based Interviewing, each question is deliberately designed to obtain behavioral examples to assess the candidate's competence in a particular job-related area. Questions are crafted so that candidates give real-life examples using what are called "SAR statements" (S = the situation in which the behavior took place, A = the action the candidate took to address the situation, R = the results of the action). Your goal is to determine not only that candidates can do what they claim they can do, but that they have actually done it and that they can describe specific situations they faced, the actions they took, and the results of their actions. A candidate must describe in detail how he handled a situation in the past, rather than just telling you what he would do in that situation or what he thinks you want to hear. Candidates must answer Behavior-Based questions factually. With Behavior-Based questions, you are probing for the end results of the situation and what the candidate's role was in achieving those results. By asking structured, open-ended, and probing questions, you will prompt candidates to reveal the necessary information you need to confidently predict how they will perform on the job.

The most reliable indicator of a candidate's future success is demonstrated proficiency in that skill through specific current and past examples. Suppose you are looking for a customer service representative who can deal with difficult customers in a fast-paced environment. You would be able to accurately assess a candidate's ability if she could describe to you several specific situations in which she actually had to deal with difficult customers, in each case describing the situation, the actions she took to address the problem, and what happened as a result. Key skills of which you would seek specific examples might include handling upset customers, taking initiative, working through problems quickly, and providing superior customer service. The candidate who was successful at solving customer problems yesterday, last month, last year, and consistently over time can certainly do it again.

A successful track record is the best job recommendation you can get, and determining how a candidate has behaved in the past with real-life examples is the heart of the Behavior-Based Interview. The key goal of an interview should therefore be to uncover a candidate's past experiences relative to predetermined competencies needed for job success. With some preplanning and structure, Behavior-Based Interview questions can be developed that allow you to scratch beneath the surface of a candidate's background.

When you use Behavior-Based Interviewing, your interviews can be well structured, and you can rest assured that your interview questions are relevant to the job requirements. You will eliminate hypothetical and fabricated answers through the use of effective probing questioning in which candidates are pinned down to talk about exactly what they did, not what they might do.

An effective program begins with developing key job-related competencies, writing behavior-based primary and follow-up questions to identify those competencies in candidates, conducting effective interview sessions, and evaluating and rating candidates' answers and all other data obtained.

When you are preparing to interview candidates, it is important to determine what the key success factors are for the position. These include technical knowledge and skills (what's needed to do the job), behaviors and performance skills (what's needed to do the job above and beyond technical knowledge), and motivations (whether a candidate *wants* to do the job). It's equally important to discover if a candidate's needs, skills, and values are such that the candidate will ultimately be a good fit for both the job and the company. Collectively, these are all referred to as competencies. Each key competency that is determined to be important for a particular job should be assessed through several Behavior-Based Interview questions. This assessment will allow you to uncover exactly how a candidate has performed in situations similar to those that will be encountered in the job under consideration. Competencies might include leadership, persuasiveness, innovative thinking, planning and organization, problem solving, and adaptability, as well as the specific technical skills defined for that position. Beyond knowledge and capabilities, your questions should be designed to learn a candidate's values and whether they will be a match for your company's values, culture, and mission. For example, you will want to clarify the type of environment that is prevalent at your company. If it is highly unstructured with a lot of change, someone who needs structure and is uncomfortable with change would not be a good fit. In Chapter 4 you will find 401 interview questions and 50 competency areas that cover technical skills, performance skills, and motivational factors. This resource, combined with Chapter 3's easy five-step process for conducting Behavior-Based Interviews, gives you both the structure and the tools you'll need to convert Behavior-Based Interviewing theory to practical reality.

It's also important to ask Behavior-Based questions that will provide you with information about negative outcomes so that you can uncover a candidate's weaknesses, past mistakes, and liabilities. A good interviewer needs to identify how a candidate performs in unfavorable and adverse situations. As an example, a question to determine a candidate's listening skills might be, "We've all had occasions when we misinterpreted something a customer told us. Tell me about a time when this happened to you." The goal is to gain well-rounded data about a candidate in a variety of circumstances. With persistence and the right line of questioning, candidates will begin to reveal both positive and negative aspects of themselves. A good sampling of questions designed to elicit negative outcomes is included among the 401 questions in Chapter 4.

If you understand how human nature works, you can really begin to understand why Behavior-Based Interviewing is so successful in predicting future performance. If you ask a candidate a hypothetical question, the hypothetical answer that you get can be developed rather quickly and more than likely will be the answer that the candidate believes you want to hear. However, when you ask a candidate for a specific example, he has to access his memory bank to determine how he handled a particular situation in the past or make up a story on the spot. Fabricating

Fifteen Reasons to Integrate Behavior-Based Interviewing into Your Hiring Practices

1. *Ease of implementation.* Chapter 3 provides an easy-to-use, step-by-step guide on how to implement Behavior-Based Interviewing so that you can begin to use it immediately. Chapter 4 has sample questions to get you started.

2. *Accuracy.* Research proves that Behavior-Based Interviewing is more valid than other interviewing methods because it more accurately predicts a candidate's potential for success.

3. *Structure.* Following a structured process with preplanned questions and objective ratings increases reliability, efficiency, and consistency.

4. *Confidence.* You can have confidence in your ability to recognize top performers through an effective hiring process that allows you to make thoughtful hiring decisions.

5. *Factual basis.* You can make more intelligent and informed hiring decisions by gathering meaningful data and facts during interviews so that you don't have to fall back on gut feelings, opinions, subjective impressions, or attitudes.

6. *No more playing amateur psychologist.* With Behavior-Based Interviewing, you can easily cite evidence about a candidate's ability to do a job once you've gathered the facts. No longer do you have to play amateur psychologist, analyzing, for example, what a candidate says about his teamwork skills or leadership style to get a clue to his overall motivations.

7. *Relevance.* Questions are designed to evaluate only those competencies that are required for success on the job. This prevents you from assessing irrelevant knowledge or skills.

8. *Preparation.* By using the behavior-based system, you will prepare a list of questions in advance, so you can control the conversation flow and collect exactly the information you need to make a decision.

9. *Cost savings.* Behavior-Based Interviewing reduces hiring mistakes because it has been proven to be more valid and it reduces costly turnover.

10. *Better fit.* You can achieve a better fit between new employees and your organization's culture by asking the right questions.

11. *Flexibility.* You determine how to integrate Behavior-Based Interview questions into your current interviewing practices, what questions to ask, what job competencies to highlight, and how to integrate this interviewing methodology with other hiring tools, such as assessments.

12. *Efficiency.* Your time with candidates will be focused and effective, and by working with other interviewers, you will eliminate unnecessary overlapping questions. With practice, your preparation time will dramatically decrease.

13. *Legal soundness.* This interviewing technique assists your organization in meeting legal guidelines for fair employment practices. Interviewers gather only information that is relevant to the job, and illegal interview biases, assumptions, and preferences based on prejudices are less likely to influence hiring decisions.

14. *Positive impressions.* The way candidates are treated during the interview process is extremely important because it will determine how they talk to others about your organization. Behavior-Based Interviews help to make positive impressions on all candidates.

15. *Fairness.* All candidates are asked the same questions and are assessed against the same set of job-related competencies. They are also rated using the same method for a consistent, fair, and accurate selection of the best candidate.

a believable-sounding story on the spot and also telling you what you want to hear is nearly impossible to do, especially when you ask for several related examples with lots of follow-up questions.

Many candidates are excellent at interviewing, having practiced their answers to traditional and hypothetical questions. They hope to get a job offer by describing what they would do once they are hired, problems they could solve, and skills they would develop. This hypothetical yet positive-sounding information may lead the inexperienced interviewer into believing that the candidate is more qualified to do the job than he or she really is. Behavior-Based Interviewing eliminates this risk.

Other Types of Interviews

There are four widely used interview types: traditional, situational, case, and behavior-based.

Traditional interviews tend to focus on questions that are leading or are résumé- and background-based. Examples are, "Tell me about yourself," "What are your strengths?" "What are your weaknesses?" "Why should we hire you?" "Where do you want to be in five years?" "Why do you want to work for us?" "Do you have sales experience?" Leading questions may hint at the answer the interviewer is looking for. An example of a leading question might be, "You're okay working under pressure in a multitasking environment, aren't you?" In a traditional interview, candidates usually provide well-rehearsed answers that they think the interviewer wants to hear.

Situational questions put candidates into hypothetical situations; they may start out with "How would . . . ?" or "What would you do if . . . ?" An example question is, "What would you do if you had an employee who was consistently late for work?" Traditional questions are asked as a way to get to know a candidate, and situational questions are often asked to test a candidate's thought processes and logical thinking, as candidates can project what they might do in a certain situation.

Case interviews are most often used by consulting firms to demonstrate how a candidate thinks and how she would go about solving a problem. The interviewer presents the candidate with a hypothetical case and asks the candidate to think out loud so that the direction of her thinking is understood. She is asked to analyze the problem, ask pertinent questions, evaluate the situation, and propose solutions and conclusions.

If you have experience with these interviewing techniques, you will find the Behavior-Based Interview different in several ways:

- You ask the candidate to describe how he actually *did* behave in a particular situation, rather than how he *would* behave.
- You ask an initial question and then follow up with several probing questions. Like a news reporter, you are digging to get to the core of the story.
- You ask the candidate for details so that she can't theorize, fabricate, or generalize answers.
- The interview is a structured process focusing on predetermined competencies, giving you more control and direction so that you don't go off course with irrelevant conversation.
- You take structured notes to document facts so that later you can rate all of your candidates accurately against consistent standards.

In traditional, situational, and case interviews, candidates have minimal accountability. How do you know that a candidate would really act the way she says she would? In a Behavior-Based Interview, it's almost impossible for a candidate to give false responses. The skilled interviewer will pick a candidate's responses apart to get at a specific behavior. The interviewer will probe further for more depth with questions such as, "What was your reasoning at this point?" or "Tell me more about the obstacles you were facing," or "Lead me through your thought process." If a candidate tells a truthful story, her answers will hold up through the bombardment of probing questions.

As an example, if you ask hypothetically what a candidate would do if he were given more tasks than he could handle, the candidate could reply by saying that he would delegate those tasks to his team as necessary. But if you ask the candidate for a specific example, you will get a real-life situation along with details about how the candidate handled that situation. Then you can ask probing questions to verify what the candidate has told you. For example, you can ask the candidate to take you through the actual steps of how he resolved the situation and what the final results were.

Enhancing Other Interview Types with Behavior-Based Interviewing

More and more organizations are moving away from using just traditional and situational interviewing questions toward a Behavior-Based Interviewing approach, or at least toward using a combination. It's easy to see how you can greatly enhance a traditional interview with behavior-based techniques. When traditional interviewing questions are the only methodology, success rates can be dismally low, especially if the interview is unstructured and not planned out in advance. Behavior-Based Interviewing is a vast improvement because it provides a way to obtain a more objective set of facts to make important employment decisions.

Even if your company has chosen not to adopt Behavior-Based Interviewing as its formal structure and process, you as an interviewer can incorporate Behavior-Based questions into the traditional interviews that your company prefers. Such questions will give you better information about a candidate and allow you to more accurately and consistently assess a slate of candidates to find the person whose skills, competencies, track record, motivators, and goals best fit the position and your organization.

Begin by asking traditional questions to gather background information. This can be the "get to know the candidate" phase. As you move into more specific questions related to the job under consideration, supplement your traditional and situational questions with behavior-based probes. For example, if you ask the traditional question, "What are your strengths?" follow up that query with a Behavior-Based question that gives you insight into one of the key qualifications for the job. If the candidate tells you that a key strength is "teamwork," and if this is an important skill for the position, you can say, "Tell me about a time when you developed a group into a strong working team." Probe for more specific information by asking questions such as "How did you get involved?" "What did you do?" "How did it turn out?" "What did you say?" "What did he/she say?" or "What happened next?"

Be sure to enhance your interview preparation by preselecting appropriate questions from Chapter 4 or developing your own questions modeled on the examples.

This informal addition of Behavior-Based questions will yield valuable information. It is not as consistent, fair, or effective as a formal, structured Behavior-Based Interviewing program implemented companywide, but perhaps this is beyond your control. In that case, you can use these techniques to enhance your own hires, and down the road, once you have a record of good hires from using these methods, you can champion the adoption of a formal program.

Interview Examples

Next you will find three separate examples of interviews. Each case presents a traditional and then a behavior-based set of questions. In the traditional interview examples, you will see that the candidate's answers are hypothetical and opinion-based and fail to sustain his claims. In each Behavior-Based example, on the other hand, the interviewer is able to obtain rich, detailed information. Compare the two examples in each case and you will see the differences. By combining the traditional and behavior-based lines of questioning, in all three cases the interviewer would be in a better position to make a more accurate hiring decision. If someone asks the interviewer why she believes a candidate would be a good hire, she will be able to cite specific examples of relevant past performance that she was able to obtain through Behavior-Based questioning.

Example I

Traditional Interview

Competency: Customer service

Interviewer: What would you do if you had a difficult customer situation?

Candidate: I would try to find out what the problem was and then see if there was anything that I could do to help out. After I helped to solve the problem, I would find out whether the customer was satisfied.

Interviewer: Do you feel that you have strong customer service skills?

Candidate: Yes. I am confident and comfortable with the relationships that I have with my customers. I understand their challenges and expectations.

Behavior-Based Interview

The following example asks the same questions behaviorally.

Competency: Customer service

Interviewer: Give me a specific example of when you had to work with a difficult customer.

Candidate: I was an agent working for an insurance company when I received a telephone call from a lady who was very upset with our company. As soon as I said hello, she started yelling at me. She didn't care who I was. She just went on and on for well over a minute, complaining about the company and how we were crooks. I finally had a chance to break into the conversation, and I asked her if I could ask her a couple of questions. She spouted off some more, and then I told her that I wanted to help her. I said that I understood that she was upset and that I wanted to solve her problem. "Would you allow me to do that?" I asked.

Interviewer: What did you do next?

Candidate: I asked her a series of questions and found out that she was upset with another agent. He had given her a quote on her auto policy, and it came back much more expensive. I pulled up her information and went over her insurance coverage with her. I reviewed her claim activity from her prior carrier, which included a claim that we had to charge her by law. I explained that to her and told her that we wanted her business and that this charge would come off her insurance record by renewal time if she just stayed with us. And, her increased premium would also decrease at that time. I asked her if she was willing to do that.

Interviewer: What did she say?

Candidate: She finally calmed down and said yes. This situation was partly her fault because she hadn't told us about her previous tickets and accidents. But if I had told her that if she should just have been up front with the first agent about this, that would have made her even more angry.

Interviewer: What was the outcome?

Candidate: Not only did she stay with us, but she switched from the other agent to me, and she also brought other business to me.

This behavior-based example shows you how to follow up with probing questions. Your objective is to have a clear representation of how the candidate actually behaved in a specific situation. You can see by this example that the candidate has superior customer service skills based on this detailed story of previous performance with a very upset customer.

Example 2

Traditional Interview

Competency: Leadership

Interviewer: Are you considered a good leader?

Candidate: Yes. The people who work under me have come to me and commented that they thought I was really good as a manager.

Interviewer: What are your strengths?

Candidate: I can quickly assess variables, and I'm a pretty quick study.

Behavior-Based Interview

Competency: Leadership

Interviewer: Tell me about a situation in which you had to lead many people to achieve a goal.

Candidate: When I was a sales manager, we had had a good year in sales the previous year, and several people in my group were trying to vie for recognition individually. I pulled them together in a group and told them that we operate as a unit and that we will be better as a collective unit than we would be individually. I told them if we work together, the whole group will be a star group, and people will begin to notice them individually.

Interviewer: How did they respond?

Candidate: At first, some of them looked like deer caught in head-lights. But over time, they embraced the idea and really started to support each other.

Interviewer: How did you keep the momentum going?

Candidate: I developed a mentor program. The people in the group who were more senior and more experienced were teamed with those in the group who had less experience. It was their responsibility to talk on a weekly basis to address the little things in between. I called these the "cracks" that the mentor can help to fill. I made the mentors accountable and reviewed their performance in this area during their quarterly reviews. Everyone understood that their destiny was tied together because everyone had ownership of the entire group.

Interviewer: What was the outcome?

Candidate: My team went from being number 23 in the country to being number 1 in the country in less than 12 months. All the team members were very proud of what they had accomplished.

You can see that when she is asked these types of questions, the candidate cannot make up the information or give hypothetical answers about what she might do.

Example 3

Traditional Interview

Competency: Persuasion

Interviewer: Are you able to persuade others?

Candidate: Most of the time I can. If there is a difference of opinions, I let the other party lay out their point of view first. I'll then lay out my point of view and come back and argue what doesn't make sense. That's how I persuade people.

Behavior-Based Interview

Competency: Persuasion

Interviewer: Describe a situation in which you were able to use persuasion to successfully convince someone to see things your way or to do something.

Candidate: I was working in our corporate offices at the time. My company had purchased a whole company in California, and we had put a vice president there to run things. I was given to this vice president as a resource from the home office. We had lots of conversations, and he asked me what I could do to help his organization. I developed a plan to help the two companies' independent contractors—benefits specialists and agents—work together. He had tried his best to develop a business arrangement between the two entities, but it didn't work. The agents didn't believe it was worth their time, and they didn't see any financial benefits. I asked him for $40,000 and told him that I would develop a program that would more than make up for the $40,000.

Interviewer: How did he react to that?

Candidate: He bought the idea after I developed a business case that showed him how the business-to-business relationships could work profitably over time. I wrote it out and explained the payback and the return on investment. I kept it simple so that he could understand the terms.

Interviewer: What was the end result?

Candidate: Once we rolled out the program, the business relationships increased tenfold across the country, and revenue increased by $7 million in less than 6 months.

Compared with the situational example given first, the second response gives compelling evidence of this candidate's ability to persuade someone to his point of view. Notice how the interviewer continued to probe until the full SAR (Situation-Action-Result) story was revealed.

These examples clearly illustrate how powerful, informative, and effective the responses to Behavior-Based Interview questions are. The information that is gained provides meaningful insight into a candidate's capabilities and allows the interviewer to make an informed judgment about the candidate's ability to perform in the new job.

Results

Companies that have implemented Behavior-Based Interviewing and tracked the results are reporting impressive success stories. As an example, Golden Corral, a nationwide restaurant chain, lowered its annual turnover of general managers from nearly 60 percent to single digits, reducing its annual costs of hiring replacements by more than $3 million in 18 months after the implementation of Behavior-Based Interviewing techniques.

Exercise—A Quiz on Interview Questions

Test your knowledge of the different types of interview questions. Identify the type of question that each of the following represents—traditional, situational, or behavior-based.

_____ 1. How would you resolve a customer service problem where the customer demanded an immediate refund?

_____ 2. Give me an example of when you had a customer service problem and the customer demanded an immediate refund.

_____ 3. Tell me about a time when you had to juggle a number of work priorities. What did you do?

_____ 4. You can work weekends occasionally, can't you?

_____ 5. What is your idea of the perfect job?

_____ 6. What would you do if you had to work with someone who was difficult to get along with?

_____ 7. What is your management style?

_____ 8. Describe a situation that you had to solve without much guidance.

_____ 9. Have you ever missed a deadline?

_____ 10. Give me an example of a situation in which you failed to make a sale because you did not understand the information provided to you by a sales prospect.

Answer Key

1. Situational
2. Behavior-Based
3. Behavior-Based
4. Traditional (leading)
5. Traditional
6. Situational
7. Traditional
8. Behavior-Based
9. Traditional
10. Behavior-Based

The Behavior-Based Interview in Five Easy Steps

I am convinced that nothing we do is more important than hiring and developing people. At the end of the day you bet on people, not on strategies.
—Larry Bossidy

I N THIS CHAPTER you will learn the five steps to conducting successful interviews, and you can implement these steps immediately. After reading this chapter, you will be able to:

- Plan and conduct controlled interview sessions
- Develop Behavior-Based questions
- Acquire evidence of job success factors in candidates
- Rate your candidates in a highly reliable way based on job-related data
- Make your hiring decisions with confidence

The five-step process includes:

Step 1   Define what you're looking for—understand the job and
         the company

Step 2   Identify job-related success factors

Step 3   Establish questions to extract the desired success factors

Step 4   Conduct a successful interview

Step 5   Perform a final evaluation—rate the evidence

Step 1: Define What You're Looking for— Understand the Job and the Company

Conducting a successful Behavior-Based Interview requires understanding the open position as well as the company's values, goals, and unique culture. Step 1 involves gathering information about the open position to identify the activities that make up the job—the required technical skills and knowledge, and also the behaviors and performance skills that must be present in a top-performing employee. Reviewing job descriptions, performance appraisals, and business plans is a good place to start your research. If a job description does not currently exist, create one that defines the skill requirements, job responsibilities, and top priorities for that position.

How to Prepare and Use Job Descriptions

There are many benefits to having a well-written job description and a clear understanding of what you are looking for in a candidate. The hiring process will run smoothly and you will virtually eliminate misunderstandings between recruiters, hiring managers, and candidates if everyone is on the same page. When a job description is shared with a candidate who is ultimately hired, that person will know exactly what is expected from day one, especially if the job description takes future developments into account. If you clearly understand the job requirements, you can easily eliminate unqualified candidates during the screening process and invite only qualified candidates for the interviewing phase.

TIP: It's important that you understand your company's specific procedures for developing job descriptions and follow them carefully. If well-written job descriptions are standard practice at your company, you can skip the section, "How to Prepare and Use Job Descriptions." We have provided it to guide those readers who need to build their knowledge of how to develop job descriptions and use them as part of the hiring process.

A job description typically includes these sections:

1. *Heading.* A summary of the open position—the job title, whom the position reports to, job titles reporting to the position, division or department name, geographic location, salary grade, employment status, travel requirements, and date.
2. *Position purpose.* A few sentences describing the objective of the position, major accomplishments, and why the position exists.
3. *Duties and responsibilities.* A list of essential job functions describing what has to be done to achieve the desired results.
4. *Qualifications.* A description of the minimum requirements for performing the essential functions. This section might include required education and experience, special skills, and certifications.
5. *Other.* Some job descriptions include other categories such as the physical requirements of a job, other departments that this employee will be expected to work with, and measurable performance standards.

Exhibit 3-1 is a sample job description for an open marketing manager position. To begin developing your own job description, use the blank Job Description Worksheet found in Appendix 2. Distribute copies of the Job Description Worksheet to managers, human resource representatives, and anyone else involved in your hiring process. Have them fill out the worksheet and return it to you, then use the information in these worksheets to write the job description. Send your final draft for approval to all those who gave you input, and remind them to think about any future developments that might affect this position. Business plans and forecasted goals can also assist in planning for future job requirements.

Ways to Determine What the Position Requires

Examine your company by gathering its mission statement, values and guiding principles, and competitive advantage statements. Check with the human resources, investor relations, and marketing departments for this information. Don't just assume that you know your company's mission and values because you've been working there a long time. Perhaps the company's focus has changed because of a new advertising campaign, a merger or acquisition, or a threat in the marketplace. For example, a company's values might include integrity, innovation, teamwork, and a high degree of customer focus and satisfaction.

Exhibit 3-1 Job Description Worksheet Example

ABC Company

JOB SPECIFICS

Position Title:	*Marketing manager*
Reports To:	*Director of sales and marketing*
Supervises:	*Writers, designers, and project coordinators*
Division/Department:	*Communication Services*
Location:	*San Francisco, California*
Salary Grade:	*12*
Employment Status:	*Regular full-time*
Travel:	*25% overnight travel*
Date:	*Month/Day/Year*

POSITION PURPOSE

Manages the marketing communications function and creates and implements marketing strategies that promote the company's products and services to customers and prospects, resulting in revenue generation and superior customer satisfaction.

DUTIES AND RESPONSIBILITIES

1. *Consults with product marketing and sales departments to develop and implement marketing plans to meet revenue goals.*

2. *Develops competitive advantage strategies to address specific market needs by identifying industry trends and competitive threats.*

3. *Plans and implements projects in advertising, sales collateral, sales training and tools, public relations, trade shows, customer events, and Internet marketing.*

4. *Manages the consistency of marketing messages and develops sales proposals.*

5. *Has overall responsibility for supervising the marketing team.*

QUALIFICATIONS

1. *Bachelor's degree in marketing or a closely related field.*

2. *Minimum 7 years' experience in marketing and 2 years in direct sales.*

3. *Minimum 2 years' experience working with customer relationship management (CRM) software.*

4. *Proven track record in analyzing the marketplace, establishing revenue targets, and meeting and exceeding those targets.*

5. *Demonstrated ability to lead teams, prioritize work schedules, and multitask.*

6. *Strong written and verbal communications.*

7. *Ability to work in a fast-paced, ever-changing environment.*

8. *Creative and innovate with the ability to see the big picture.*

9. *Experience in the financial services industry preferred.*

It's equally important that you have a complete understanding of your company's environment. Is it lean and mean, big and bureaucratic, or somewhere in between? Gathering job descriptions, business plans, company mission statements, and company values and having a clear picture of the working environment will help you determine whether a candidate is the best fit for the job and for the company.

Step 2: Identify Job-Related Success Factors

Now that you've performed your research, it's time to establish the "success factors" for this job.

Distribute your material to the people who know the position best. This might include employees who have previously held or are currently holding the position, fellow team members and supervisors of the position,

TIP: Review the performance appraisals of your top employees in the same or similar positions. Look for exceptional performance—times when employees have taken ownership, shown commitment, and gone above and beyond expectations—and consider what actions those top performers took to get there.

others who interact with the position, human resources representatives, and any other key stakeholders. Invite this team to a group session with the goal of defining job competencies or success factors for these categories:

- Skills, including:
  - Technical knowledge and skills
    Technical knowledge and skills consist of specialized competencies that are required for the job, such as marketing knowledge or knowledge of a particular software program. Technical knowledge may come from work experience, education, credentials, or certifications.
  - Performance skills
    Better known as behaviors, *performance skills* are those abilities above and beyond technical knowledge that are needed to do the job. Examples of performance skills include leadership, initiative, attention to detail, and persuasiveness.
- Motivations (including job fit and company fit)
  Motivations reveal whether a person *will* do the job, not just whether the person *can* do it. Identifying motivations is critical for matching a candidate's preferred working environment with what is present in the job and at the company.

Asking others to help you define the key competencies is important. The team will help validate the competencies and success factors, and you will build a greater consensus about and acceptance of the overall hiring process. When inviting the key players to your group session, let them know that you want to learn how an employee can be successful in your open position, and that you need their assistance in identifying what it takes to achieve excellence. Prepare for your group session by giving each member a list of questions. The following is a list of sample questions that you can hand out to help your group determine the key

TIP: A further explanation of skills and motivations is provided later in this step, when we walk you through the process of creating a Job Competency Chart. These concepts are very easy to grasp and will quickly help you become proficient at zeroing in on the key skills and motivators for each position.

competencies required for each specific job you have. You might also wish to use the 50 distinct competencies we have identified in Chapter 4, along with sample questions for each, as a resource.

Questions to Identify Key Job Competencies

1. Identify the position's current and future required knowledge and technical skills.
2. Identify other current and future skills that are required.
3. Identify other behaviors and performance skills that are necessary for top performance.
4. What factors distinguish a top performer from an average performer?
5. What is unique about the department's environment that will affect the open position, and what attributes are needed to be successful in that environment?
6. What important values that correspond with the company's values and mission statement is it critical to have?
7. What else does the company wish to be known for? What are the competitive advantages?
8. What is the company's overall environment, and what attributes are needed to be successful in that environment?
9. What other organizational strengths are required for top performance?
10. Will there be new roles established based on future business demands? What else is important to consider?

TIP: Keep it simple by identifying the "must-have" competencies that define exceptional behavior, and narrow those down to the top 10 to 12. Identify the actions taken to achieve top-performance results, such as what it takes to bring in extraordinary revenue for a sales position or how to consistently reach off-the-charts customer satisfaction scores if the job is in customer service. Define the results you are looking for and the "perfect person profile" when developing your list of competencies. It's just as important to recognize what's happening in your company, your industry, and the marketplace so that you can address current and upcoming issues that may be relevant.

Begin the group session by reviewing your research materials and answering questions similar to the sample questions just shown. Develop a Job Competency Chart by identifying each competency and the top-performance actions or proficiencies required that are unique to your organization and the way you do business. The Job Competency Chart will also be the basis for creating Behavior-Based Interview questions in step 3.

A Job Competency Chart for our marketing manager example is shown in Exhibit 3-2, and a chart for you to use is included in Appendix 2.

The Job Competency Chart—Column I

The first column of the Job Competency Chart lists the standard competency categories—*skills* (*technical knowledge and skills* and *performance skills*—better known as behaviors) and *motivations* (*job fit* and *company fit*). Recall that technical knowledge and skills are the specialized competencies that are required for the job. Technical knowledge may come from work experience, education, credentials, or certifications.

Beyond technical knowledge are the performance skills, or behaviors, that are needed to do the job. Behaviors that are important for our marketing manager example include strategic planning, leadership, planning and organizing, and innovation.

Motivations reveal whether a candidate not only can do the job but will do the job. Motivational fit is extremely important. In fact, job dissatisfaction is the number-one reason that employees voluntarily leave their jobs. Conversely, a highly motivated employee who enjoys his or her job will demonstrate a high level of dedication and energy, exhibit a positive "can do" attitude, and consistently strive to achieve and surpass the desired results.

Develop pointed interview questions to identify each candidate's motivations. These questions might encompass job-related likes and dislikes, causes for satisfaction, and reasons for dissatisfaction in past positions and organizations. (A list of motivational-fit questions can be found in Chapter 4.) Identify what motivates each candidate, and compare that information to what the candidate will find in your open position (job fit) and your organization (company fit). It's important to ensure that a new hire's needs for money, recognition, development and training, achievement, challenge, promotion, and a wide variety of tasks,

Exhibit 3-2 Job Competency Chart Example

Competency Category	Competency Name	Top Performance Actions/ Proficiency Required
SKILLS		
Technical Knowledge and Skills	Sales	• Two years in direct sales, achieving 100 percent of quota.
	Marketing	• Bachelor's degree in marketing or related field. • Minimum 7 years' marketing experience. • Strong ability to plan and execute major marketing campaigns.
	Customer relationship management (CRM) software	• Minimum 2 years' experience in developing CRM software sales training and tools.
Behaviors (performance skills)	Strategic planning	• Comprehends the "big picture," accurately assesses opportunities and marketplace threats, and develops action plans to combat threats.
	Leadership	• Motivates by example and fosters a positive working environment.
	Planning and organizing	• Plans, organizes, and schedules multiple tasks and projects to staff members; ensures that projects are completed on time and within budget.
	Innovation	• Develops new product solutions to increase revenue and customer loyalty.
MOTIVATIONS		
Job Fit	Adaptability	• Adjusts quickly to changing priorities and copes well with complexity.
Company Fit	Customer focus	• Establishes partner relationships with internal and external customers. • Provides satisfaction that goes beyond expectations.
	Integrity	• Earns and maintains trust of company employees and clients. • Puts company interests first.

for example, are compatible with the opportunities the job has to offer and what your company can provide.

Job-fit and company-fit competencies should be tailored toward the special characteristics of your organization. Asking interview questions aimed at matching a candidate's values and preferences with your company's values, mission, environment, and usual mode of operation will ensure an overall good fit and a highly motivated employee.

The Job Competency Chart—Column 2

The second column of the Job Competency Chart is where you list the specific competencies that you have identified for each of the competency categories. Keep your list to 12 competencies or less so that you don't reduce the effectiveness of your interview sessions. If there are other competencies that you've identified as important, design Behavior-Based questions around those competencies to ask candidates during a second round of interviews if necessary (we discuss how to formulate these questions in the next step). When identifying competencies, remember that they should be quantifiable, measurable, and able to be replicated.

The Job Competency Chart—Column 3

The third category of the Job Competency Chart includes top-performance actions, which are short descriptions of how to do the job successfully, not just the "what" of the job. In the technical knowledge category, top-performance actions might also include the degree of proficiency required. You can have several top-performance actions and proficiency requirements for a job competency. Tapping into your group's knowledge of what top performers do differently will provide you with rich ideas so that you can home in on success factors and look for those during your interviews.

The key job competencies that you've identified will become the foundation for the rest of the interviewing process, and they will also provide you with an objective basis for assessing which candidates are qualified for your open position.

Step 3: Establish Questions to Extract the Desired Success Factors

To determine whether a candidate possesses the competencies identified in step 2, begin by developing Behavior-Based Interview ques-

> **TIP:** This book provides you with an extensive list of questions so that you don't have to invent them yourself. You can use the questions exactly as written, or you can use them as a model and adapt them for the specifics of your own company and the position you're filling. But if you would like to create your own Behavior-Based questions, the next paragraphs will show you how. All it takes is a little practice and a well-thought-out plan.

tions for each competency. Chapter 4 contains 50 widely used competencies and 401 interview questions—most of them behavior-based, but icebreakers and probing/follow-up questions are also included, along with traditional and situational questions for getting to know a candidate's background and testing her or his thought processes.

As we've discussed, Behavior-Based questions are open-ended and always start out with something like "Tell me about a time when . . ." or "Give me an example of . . ." or "Describe . . ." You want to generate responses in the form of SAR statements (the full situation, actions taken, and the results of the situation) so that you can rate the candidate on the job-related competencies identified. Because you're not interested in mediocre or everyday occurrences, questions are created so that candidates focus on the "best" or "most" or "greatest" situations from their past. An example of this type of question is, "Tell me about your most successful sale to a new client." Most importantly, word questions so that they address the top-performance action statements you developed in step 2.

We recommend that you use three interviewers and equip each interviewer with two or three different but similar Behavior-Based questions for each competency. At least two interviewers should ask questions covering the same competency. It's easier to compare candidates by asking them similar questions and evaluating them against the same criteria. When questions have been developed prior to the interview, interviewers are focused and prepared to ask only job-related questions, and candidates experience an organized interview that reflects positively on the company.

For the first competency category, *technical knowledge and skills*, ask questions to determine the candidate's degree of proficiency for each key competency. In our marketing manager example, marketing is a required technical skill, so you might ask, "Having the ability to plan and execute a marketing campaign to both internal and external audiences is a skill that is required. Give me an example of when you planned and executed your most successful marketing campaign. What was the situation? What were your specific actions? What were the results?" This is also an appropriate time to ask non-Behavior-Based questions to learn more about the background and depth of a candidate's technical knowledge.

The second category focuses on *behaviors and performance skills*, and this is where you want to develop structured questions to determine the presence of these behaviors. For the example marketing manager position, we've identified strategic planning, leadership, planning and organizing, and innovation as critical needs. You will find a number of sample questions covering the top-performance actions in Exhibit 3-3.

Don't forget to ask questions that reveal *contrary information* so that you can uncover both a candidate's strengths and his or her weaknesses. You can develop questions by changing a single word or phrase from a previously asked question and softening it a bit. For example, you can change the planning and organizing question, "Give me an example of when you were working on many projects at one time and they all had aggressive deadlines," to, "We've all had occasions when we missed deadlines. Give me an example of when you were working on many projects at one time and you did not meet a deadline."

It's equally important to ask questions that match the *results* you are looking for from a top performer. You may have obtained results criteria from performance appraisals, business plans, and departmental goals assessed during the research phase. For example, the performance level sought for a sales professional might be to increase revenue by 150 percent over a 12-month period through aggressive outbound calling campaigns. A good strategy is to tell the candidate the results you are looking for and then ask, "Tell me about a time when you achieved results similar to this objective."

Next, you want to develop questions to determine a candidate's own *motivations*. Ask questions to determine the candidate's preferences concerning what aspects of the job and the organization will and will not motivate her or him. Compare those preferences to the required

Exhibit 3-3 Job Competencies with Behavior-Based Questions

Competency Name	Top Performance Actions	Behavior-Based Questions
Strategic Planning	• Comprehends the "big picture," accurately assesses opportunities and marketplace threats, and develops action plans to combat threats.	• Describe a situation in which you anticipated marketplace threats and made changes to current products to meet future needs.
Leadership	• Motivates by example and fosters a positive working environment.	• Tell me about a time when morale was low and you fostered positive change in your department.
Planning and Organizing	• Plans, organizes, and schedules multiple tasks and projects to staff members; ensures that projects are completed on time and within budget.	• Give me an example of when you were working on many projects at one time and they all had aggressive deadlines. How did you handle it?
Innovation	• Develops new product solutions to increase revenue and customer loyalty.	• Describe a time when you created a new service or product.

motivating factors needed to be successful in the job. Questions to draw out revealing information include, "Why are you in marketing?" or "Tell me about the most rewarding job experience you have had. What did you like about it?" or "Tell me about a difficult task you have had. What did you dislike about it?"

You want to ensure a good *job fit* and *company fit*. In our marketing manager example, it was determined that adaptability was a key job-fit competency. Top-performance actions consisted of adjusting quickly to changing priorities. A good question to ask is, "Describe a time when you had to adjust quickly to changing priorities." Organizational fit competencies are unique to your organization and its culture. Customer focus and integrity were identified as key competencies for the marketing manager position. In this case, questions that you can ask are, "Tell me about a time when you initiated a change in response to customer feedback" and "Describe a situation when you had to handle a tough problem that challenged your integrity."

TIP: Here's an easy way to assess motivational fit for any competency you're interviewing for. When the candidate has concluded her answer in an SAR format, ask, "How satisfied/dissatisfied were you with that, and why?" You'll gain immediate and relevant clues to that individual's likes, dislikes, and preferences that can help you establish whether she is a good fit for the job. You can also ask questions about areas for which there are few or no opportunities in the job under consideration. For example, if the job offers few or no opportunities for formal recognition (such as awards, plaques, ceremonies, or bonuses), you could ask, "Tell me about a time when you received formal recognition for your work, and another time when your work was not recognized formally. How satisfied/dissatisfied were you with each of these experiences?"

Throughout your questioning, always *probe* to get the full situation and background, the actions the candidate took to solve the problem, and the end results. Ask probing or clarifying questions when you receive an incomplete answer, detect a candidate's avoidance of a response, need additional information, or do not understand a response, digging deeper to elicit the details.

With practice, a skilled interviewer can easily prepare job-related and *legally* appropriate questions. (See Chapter 6 for a review of legal guidelines.) For example, if a job requires out-of-town travel 30 percent of the time, you can't ask, "I understand you have a working spouse and children in preschool. How can you travel with this situation at home?" But you could word your question this way to get the information you need: "This job requires you to travel out of town about two days a week. Would that be a problem for you?"

It's easy to write Behavior-Based questions. Begin practicing by rewriting these questions:

Question 1: "Do you have experience in building teams?"

_____

_____

Question 2: "Do you have good customer service skills?"

_____

_____

Suggested rewrites are:

Question 1: "Tell me about a specific time when building a team was required of you."
Question 2: "Describe a situation when you had an angry customer."

Selecting questions for your interviewers should be a quick process once you have established agreed-upon competencies and motivational fit factors. Everyone involved in the hiring process will understand the position requirements, success factors, and environmental factors, and your questions will be designed to elicit evidence from the candidate's background that supports these key qualities. Remember, you will be able to use many of the questions in Chapter 4 exactly as written, or you can create your own questions based on the examples we have provided.

Step 4: Conduct a Successful Interview

Now you are ready to conduct the actual interview. You can use Behavior-Based questions, traditional, situational and case questions, or any combination during an interview. To increase your chances of finding the best candidate, we recommend that the majority of the questions you ask be Behavior-Based.

Step 4 provides you with an interview structure, interviewing tips, questioning techniques, and suggestions on how to create a relaxing and comfortable atmosphere for the candidate. On average, interviews last approximately 60 minutes. We have provided a suggested structure for your interview so that you can remain focused and on track and get the results you need to make a proper evaluation of the candidate. Your goal is to collect two to three complete SAR statements for each critical competency.

Interview Success Tips

Here is a list of our top-ten tip suggestions to ensure that you meet your interview goals.

1. *Practice, practice, and practice.* You can learn to ask behavior-based and probing questions naturally by practicing them on your peers. You will quickly learn whether you are getting the

Structuring Your Interview

Introduction (3 to 5 minutes of a 60-minute interview)

1. *Build rapport.* Always make the candidate comfortable and relaxed by using conversation openers and asking rapport-building questions. (A list of icebreaker questions is included in Chapter 4.) Show a genuine interest and give each candidate your full attention by conducting the interview in a quiet, private space with the door closed and the phones set on "do not disturb." Ask others not to interrupt you during the interview.
2. *Provide background information.* Give the candidate background information about the open position and the company.
3. *Communicate expectations.* Share with the candidate what she can expect during the interview. Inform the candidate that you will be asking questions first, that you will be taking notes, and that you will allow time at the end for her questions. Explain that you will be asking questions to get specific examples, and that in each case you want to hear about the situation, the actions the candidate took, and the end results. Mention that you will ask follow-up questions to ensure that you get the details on these three sections. Tell the candidate that it's okay if an actual situation doesn't come right to mind and that you will allow her time to tap into her memory bank or you will go back to those questions later. Ask the candidate if she has any questions before you continue.

Interviewer's Questions / Candidate's Answers
(45 minutes of a 60-minute interview)

This is the part of the interview where you will be doing most of your data gathering, so take good notes. Many interviews begin with background questions, using the candidate's résumé as a guide. You might plan to conduct a combination interview, starting off with traditional and non-Behavior-Based questions. Just as with Behavior-Based questions, be sure to prepare in advance the traditional and situational interview questions you will ask in the interview. We recommend that you devote the bulk of your time—at least 25 minutes—to Behavior-Based questions. Pace yourself according to the number of competencies you have identified, and remember that you want to ask two or three questions for each competency. Your objective is to find evidence that a candidate has the mandatory competencies you've identified to do the job. Make sure the candidate does most of the talking during this phase.

Candidate's Questions
(10 minutes of a 60-minute interview)

Leave enough time to answer the candidate's questions. Most candidates have prepared questions to show that they are very interested in the position.

Interview Close (3 to 5 minutes of a 60-minute interview)

1. *Sell your company.* This is the time to sell the benefits of working for your company. It's important that you treat each candidate as a customer and that you leave a positive impression of your organization.
2. *Communicate the next steps.* Candidates want to know the next steps of the interview process and when they will hear from you. Let them know what to expect, and thank them for their time.

full situation, action, and results and what probing questions to ask if you are not. Practice will help you gain confidence.

2. *Get the full story.* Some candidates may not be able to answer your questions, or their answers may be vague and incomplete. If you can't get an answer at all, use a different choice of words to restate the question, come back to the question later, or ask another question dealing with the same competency. Always maintain rapport with the candidate, be supportive, and provide guidance, because stress can interfere with a candidate's thinking and ability to respond clearly. Do not convert the question into a hypothetical question, and don't become impatient.

If, for example, you ask a candidate for a specific situation involving one of his most successful sales and he answers the question hypothetically, like this: "When I first meet with a new customer, I ask a lot of questions to determine what their needs and challenges are," you can politely stop him and get him back on track by responding, "That's a great strategy. Can you give me a specific example of how you won over a customer?"

Listen for clues that you may be getting vague answers. These include the use of "we" instead of "I"; not using past-tense action verbs (saying "I always" or "I would" instead of "I developed" or "I led"); not providing actual dates, times, names, places, or specifics; and answering questions hypothetically and theoretically. In these cases, probe with follow-up questions such as, "What role did you actually play?" or "What specifically was your involvement?" This will allow you to determine how much the candidate contributed to the situation.

If you get incomplete answers, continue probing for the situation, action, and results. Ask for another example to gather even more evidence. If a candidate can't provide you with a satisfactory answer even after probing, move on. Candidates can't invent specific examples in a short period of time, so you can quickly determine whether or not they have the required competency.

3. *Handling silence.* When you ask a Behavior-Based question, you may hear nothing while the candidate thinks. Let the silence go on for about five to ten seconds before defusing the situation. It will help if you talk about the possibility of silence early on and mention that you understand that coming up with specific situations may take some thought. It's very different from having preplanned answers to questions.

4. *Use prepared questions.* Your prepared questions will provide structure to your interview and allow you to treat all candidates fairly. By asking every candidate the same questions, you can accurately compare the candidates with one another and ensure a legal selection process.

5. *Control the interview.* The goal of the interview is to gather as much job-related data as possible in a short period of time and to ensure that irrelevant discussions do not occur. It's appropriate to guide the candidate during the interview, prompting him to continue talking, change subjects, or make a point. A good strategy is to use tactful interruptions with the candidate's name, a clarification, and a new, probing question. Here's an example: "That's very interesting, Lee, and I really like your enthusiasm. But I want to be sure we talk about all of the different areas of your background that relate to this position. With regard to the wireless project, can you tell me precisely what role you played in the rollout?"

6. *Probe for information.* So that the candidate expects follow-up questions, explain that you will be probing for information to get the situation, action, and results. Even the best candidate will need guidance. Candidates don't naturally provide specific behavior-based examples in an interview. The questions should

always be asked conversationally and in a manner that makes the candidate comfortable, so she doesn't feel that she is being interrogated.

7. *Evaluate candidates after the interview.* Behavior-Based Interviews are geared toward gathering job-related facts during the questions and documenting those facts by taking notes. Making evaluations and prejudgments during the interview is premature and takes away from effective listening. Write down what you hear so that you can make an evaluation after all the facts are in. Don't judge a candidate because she can't come up with an example right away.

8. *Take descriptive notes.* Listen carefully to a candidate's responses and reflect exactly what is said by taking good, factual notes. Taking good notes will help you rate the presence of competencies later on and help you distinguish one candidate from another. Stick to the facts—don't write down your opinions, impressions, or interpretations of what you believe a candidate said. It's also important to take detailed notes because they are your documentation of the reasons for your hiring choices. Write your notes in the correct situation/action/results sections of your Interview Guide (see Exhibit 3-4). A bad example of note taking is, "Candidate is knowledgeable and had several examples that she could recall with ease." You will have great difficulty rating this candidate on the basis of these notes. Instead, put down brief details of each part of the SAR story to be certain that you have captured the full situation, action, and result; ask probing questions if the candidate omits information. And be certain that you link the SAR response to the appropriate competency. Sometimes a Behavior-Based question will elicit answers that cover more than one competency, and at other times a candidate might misinterpret the question or provide a SAR that is not responsive to that question but applies to another competency area.

9. *Have three interviewers and evaluators.* It is recommended that candidates be interviewed by three interviewers who ask prepared Behavior-Based questions on the must-have set of competencies. Each interviewer should have two or three questions prepared for each competency. These questions should be similar to but not exactly the same as yours so that ratings and assessments are done consistently. Interviewers should compare

their ratings and discuss any discrepancies. Having more than one interviewer also helps control for personal biases.

10. *Follow the same guidelines in a second interview.* If a candidate looks like a possible fit for the job, invite him back for a second interview or have him continue the process by meeting with at least two other well-prepared interviewers. Ask additional questions about the most important competencies, other important competencies you didn't have time to get to previously, or competencies you've already asked questions about but for which you would like further evidence.

Using the Interview Guide

The Interview Guide is an easy-to-use tool containing all the information you need to conduct a successful interview. A sample template for you to use can be found in Appendix 2. The Interview Guide begins with a job summary that encompasses reporting relationships, responsibilities, qualifications, and measurable performance standards and goals, followed by a competency chart on which you can list the top 10 to 12 competencies and keep track of which interviewers are assigned each competency. Next comes the Skills/Competencies section. A separate page is used for each competency; two or three prepared interview questions are listed, and space is allowed for interviewers to record their notes, broken out by the situation, actions, and results. We've also provided space for you to record the candidate's response to the motivational-fit question that you can use as a follow-up to every question: "How satisfied/dissatisfied were you with that?" Next comes the Motivations section, including space for Behavior-Based questions to determine candidate motivators, and then additional competency sheets so that you can capture SARs related to job fit and company fit. In the event that you wish to ask additional situational, traditional, or case interview questions, we have provided a page for these in the Interview Guide. And for at-a-glance review, we have included a page on which you can summarize the questions asked by each interviewer to test each competency. The last section of the Interview Guide contains a rating sheet for each competency and a rating summary sheet for making a decision (see step 5 for details). All interviewers should have copies of the Interview Guide customized with their specific questions.

To illustrate how easy it is to customize and use the Interview Guide, we have created a sample competency page showing three pre-pared Behavior-Based Interview questions for the competency "strategic planning" (see Exhibit 3-4). You will recognize the competency and its top-performance actions from our earlier discussion of the marketing manager position. We selected the questions directly from the 401 sample questions in Chapter 4.

Step 5: Perform a Final Evaluation—Rate the Evidence

To evaluate candidates accurately, you must have a consistent and reliable rating system. You start by defining what is to be measured (job competencies—skills and motivations), then you gather data by interviewing a candidate and recording her situations, actions, and results for each competency. After listening carefully to a candidate's responses and taking copious notes, you are now ready to rate your findings. When the interview is complete, fill out your rating sheet immediately while your notes are still fresh in your mind. Exhibit 3-5 shows a sample rating sheet for our marketing manager example. A blank template for your use is included in Appendix 2.

To rate a candidate, compare your interview notes with your Inter-view Guide description of each competency and its high-performance actions. Keep in mind that just because a candidate has provided a com-plete SAR story that is responsive to the question does not mean she has demonstrated top performance. Be sure to focus on your expectations

> **TIP:** From time to time you may encounter candidates whose compe-tencies are well above what is required for the position. Rather than automatically dismissing them as "overqualified," simply give them a 3 for each appropriate competency and use your job-fit and company-fit motivational questions to weed out candidates who would not be satis-fied with the level of responsibility of this position. In some cases, you may find that a very qualified candidate truly desires to step down a level for greater job satisfaction. In other cases, you'll find a level of ambition and authority that signals a poor fit for the position. Follow-ing this process ensures that your hiring decisions are based on facts rather than assumptions.

Exhibit 3-4   The Interview Guide—
Skills Competency Section

PERFORMANCE SKILLS (BEHAVIORS) COMPETENCIES

Performance Skills (Behaviors) Competency: *Strategic planning*

Top Performance Action(s) Required: *Comprehends the "big picture," accurately assesses opportunities and marketplace threats, and develops action plans to combat threats*

Questions	Responses
1. *Describe a situation in which you anticipated the future and made changes to current products to meet future customer needs.*	Situation _____ _____ _____
	Actions _____ _____ _____ _____ _____
Satisfied / Dissatisfied?	
_____ _____ _____ _____	Results _____ _____ _____ _____
2. *Describe a time when there were competitive threats in your marketplace and you developed actions to compete.*	Situation _____ _____ _____
	Actions _____ _____ _____ _____ _____
Satisfied / Dissatisfied?	
_____ _____ _____ _____	Results _____ _____ _____ _____
3. *Give me an example of a time when you identified and assessed a new business opportunity.*	Situation _____ _____ _____
	Actions _____ _____ _____ _____ _____
Satisfied / Dissatisfied?	
_____ _____ _____ _____	Results _____ _____ _____ _____

Exhibit 3-5   The Interview Guide—Rating Sheet

RATING SHEET

Candidate's Name: *Robert*

Position: *Marketing manager*

Rate each competency on a scale from 1 to 3 by circling the rating.

3 = Very Strong Evidence of Desired Competency (Provided several specific and complete examples)

2 = Some Evidence of Desired Competency (Provided only one specific and complete example)

1 = No Evidence of Desired Competency (Could not provide any specific examples or provided incomplete or vague examples)

Competency Name	Rating		
Sales	1	②	3
Marketing	1	2	③
CRM software	①	2	3
Strategic planning	1	2	③
Leadership	1	②	3
Planning and organizing	1	2	③
Innovation	1	2	③
Adaptability	①	2	3
Customer focus	1	2	③
Integrity	1	2	③
	1	2	3
	1	2	3

List candidate motivators identified as a result of questioning:

Needs structured environment, not a lot of change, friendly environment, variety of work assignments with time for planning and reflection.

for this position—what do you need the employee to do, where do you need her to shine, and what kinds of examples should she provide to match the profile of a top performer in this position? Review your notes for evidence of the competency, and place your rating for each competency on the rating sheet. Look for complete SAR stories and repetitive examples of behavior, not just isolated examples. The rating sheet will help you identify the strengths and weaknesses of each candidate and how well he or she matches up to what you are looking for.

After you've rated a candidate against the mandatory competencies, review your ratings and your notes to ensure that you weren't too lenient or too tough. When you carefully adhere to the Behavior-Based Interviewing techniques outlined in this book, you will find that interviewers will closely agree on their ratings, adding reliability to this hiring method.

To make the best decision possible, all interviewers should rate the candidates separately and then get together to discuss their findings, go over their scores, and review the specific examples they have collected. Exhibit 3-6 is an example of a rating summary from three interviewers for the marketing manager position, showing the scores they assigned to the mandatory competencies. A Rating Summary template is included as part of the Interview Guide in Appendix 2.

When making a final hiring decision and comparing candidates to one another, sort the job competencies in order of importance. In Exhibit 3-6, this candidate shows no evidence of customer relationship management software skills and will have difficulty quickly adjusting to changing priorities (adaptability). If your organization is constantly changing, and if this position will greatly be affected by it, you need a candidate who can deal with those circumstances successfully.

When determining a candidate's motivations, review your notes about his likes and dislikes and what he found satisfying and dissatisfying about past and current work assignments. For example, a question to get at a candidate's motivations regarding challenging work might be, "Tell me about one of the most difficult tasks you have had. What did you like about it? What did you dislike about it?" Making a list of what the candidate liked about it will help in the rating of job fit and company fit. For example, the candidate might reveal that she dislikes details and budgetary analysis and has a strong preference for working with people. If you've identified that this job requires someone with an aptitude for detailed budgetary analysis, and you've ranked this as a

Exhibit 3-6   The Interview Guide—Rating Summary

RATING SUMMARY SHEET

Candidate's Name: _Robert_

Position: _Marketing manager_

Rate each competency on a scale from 1 to 3 by circling the rating.

3 = Very Strong Evidence of Desired Competency (Provided several specific and complete examples)

2 = Some Evidence of Desired Competency (Provided only one specific and complete example)

1 = No Evidence of Desired Competency (Could not provide any specific examples or provided incomplete or vague examples)

Record each interviewer's rating for each competency.

Summary of Ratings

Competency Name	Interviewer Name _Jane_ Rating	Interviewer Name _Dan_ Rating	Interviewer Name _Ed_ Rating
Sales	2	3	2
Marketing	3	3	3
CRM software	1	1	1
Strategic planning	3	3	3
Leadership	2	2	2
Planning and organizing	3	3	2
Innovation	3	3	3
Adaptability	1	1	1
Customer focus	3	3	3
Integrity	3	3	3

List candidate motivators identified as a result of questioning:

Needs a variety of work with time for planning and reflection, friendly environment, some freedom and independence, promotion opportunities, training and career development, recognition, structured environment, not a lot of change, likes to work with people and not on detailed analysis.

high priority, you probably shouldn't hire this candidate, even if all of her other qualifications look good.

No one candidate will be a perfect fit, so when making a final hiring decision, you must also consider other elements such as background and reference checks, salary requirements, information obtained from other assessment tools if used, and credentials.

Conclusion

It's common knowledge that you shouldn't hire someone just because that person is easygoing, friendly, or dressed professionally for the interview. Behavior-Based Interviewing allows you to evaluate candidates based on job-related elements—their technical knowledge and skills, their behaviors and performance skills, and their motivations, including job and company fit—all important indicators for doing a job at a top-performing level. Each candidate is evaluated using the very same guidelines, removing all biases and personal impressions from the equation. Candidates who go through Behavior-Based Interviews generally feel that the process demonstrates that the company is organized and is committed to hiring the best people. The process may seem more challenging to candidates and certainly more equitable.

If you plan to do additional hiring for the same position, a periodic review of the key competencies and Behavior-Based questions is all that's needed, unless the job changes often or the company's direction changes. By following the step-by-step process outlined in this chapter, and with just a little time and effort, you can significantly improve the quality of the people you hire for your organization.

Summary Checklist

The following checklist summarizes Chapter 3 by highlighting the important elements of implementing a successful Behavior-Based Interviewing process.

_____ Gather data about your open job position and your company, including job descriptions, performance appraisals, business plans, company mission statement, company values and guiding principles, and competitive advantage statements.

___ Distribute the data to those who know the open position best, along with questions to identify key competencies and top-performance activities, and invite those people to a group brainstorming session.

___ Develop key competencies as a group in the following areas: skills (technical knowledge and skills, behaviors and performance skills) and motivations (identify not just whether a candidate can do a job, but whether the candidate will do the job, and whether the candidate's motivations are a fit for the job and the company).

___ Develop at least two or three Behavior-Based questions for each competency, incorporating top-performance actions. (See Chapter 4 for examples of interview questions that you can use.) Develop questions to reveal contrary information and probing questions.

___ During the interview, establish and maintain rapport to keep the candidate at ease. Use Behavior-Based questions, probe for examples, and take good, detailed notes on the situation, action, and results of each answer.

___ Use the Interview Guide to capture the candidate's SAR stories, keep track of the questions asked by each interviewer, summarize interview findings, and record individual and group rating information.

___ Rate a candidate immediately after your interview session, while the interview is still fresh in your mind. Use your notes and rate the candidate against each competency. Compare your ratings and situation examples with the other interviewers and incorporate background and reference checks, salary requirements, information obtained from other assessment tools if used, and credentials.

___ Make your hiring decision with confidence!

401 Interview Questions

The ability to find the right question is more than half the battle of finding the answer.

—Thomas J. Watson

HERE IS THE HEART of the book: specific Behavior-Based Interview questions that you can use to predict, accurately and with confidence, a candidate's potential for success on the job.

As discussed in detail in Chapter 3, it is essential that you first identify job-related success factors (technical skills and knowledge, behaviors and performance skills, and motivations) that are matched to the essential functions of the job. You will then use Behavior-Based Interview questions to determine if the candidate has a history that demonstrates strengths and abilities in these competency areas.

We begin our sample questions with *icebreakers* that you can use during the first few minutes of greeting a candidate. Then you'll find Behavior-Based questions related to *technical skills and knowledge* and *behaviors and performance skills*. These are grouped into 50 competency areas, listed in alphabetical order. Locate the specific competency you are trying to assess, and you will find questions that you can assign to your interview team. Refer to Chapter 3 to learn how to determine which competency areas are most important in your future employee. Then search the list for the 10 or 12 you determine to be the most crucial.

Questions related to *motivations* come next. Remember, these allow you to determine that the candidate not only *can* do the job but *will* do the job. These job-fit and company-fit questions are an excellent tool for identifying the most appropriate candidate when several candidates have comparable knowledge, experience, and proficiencies. They are the key to employee satisfaction and retention.

Next, we have compiled a list of *probes* or *follow-up questions* that you can use to gather more information and ensure that you are collecting complete SAR stories.

We conclude with examples of *traditional* and *situational* questions that you can use at various points during your interviews. These are perhaps most helpful when you are gathering information related to functional capabilities. For example, it is quite valid to ask, "What is your experience with C++ programming?" You can follow up this *traditional* question with some Behavior-Based questions that will shed light on the candidate's ability to apply this experience in a team setting or under severe time pressures.

A number of questions begin with the qualifier "for managers." Designed to assess a person's ability to lead, motivate, direct, and develop staff under supervision, these questions can be used both with experienced managers and with those who have never held the title of "manager." Such candidates can share SARs about team experiences, informal or interim management roles, or mentoring relationships that will enable you to determine their ability to perform in a management position.

A critical part of the Behavior-Based Interviewing process occurs after you have selected questions and used them in candidate interviews. Members of the interview team must evaluate a slate of candidates by comparing notes and reviewing each candidate's responses. The entire process is discussed in detail in Chapter 3, from planning and preparation through interviewing, rating, and reaching consensus. Be sure you are familiar with all the steps in the process so that the Behavior-Based questions are an integral part of a well-thought-out process and not just an interesting way to get candidate information.

Breaking the Ice

Here is a resource list of introductory questions that you can ask to break the ice with candidates. Refer to Chapter 6 for important information on how to follow legal hiring practices and avoid bias even in general interview questions. Pick out the questions yourself or invite your interview team members to select the questions that they would enjoy using during the first few minutes of an interview.

Your goal with icebreaking questions is to build rapport and make candidates feel comfortable. Remember, interviewing can be a stressful situation. Candidates want to make a great impression and are anxious about answering tough questions. Ease into the conversation as you welcome the candidate, settle into comfortable seats, and begin the interview.

Icebreaking Questions

- Tell me about yourself. (This is a classic opener that many candidates have prepared for. Try to encourage the candidate to wrap up the response after a minute or so, and be careful about responding to information that might play into areas of bias—for example, if the candidate reveals that she grew up in another country or is a single parent.)
- Did you have any trouble finding our office?
- I hope you've been able to enjoy this glorious weather we're having.
- Have you been to our building before?
- I like your briefcase. Did you get it locally?
- Have you been enjoying the Olympics? (It's okay to comment on a universal event such as the Olympics or some other general current event, but don't invite discussion of local sports teams unless the team has just recently done something very notable. A nonfan might feel at a disadvantage.)
- Would you like some coffee or a glass of ice water?
- Have you ever seen downtown from this perspective?

If you have brought candidates in from other parts of the country, you might ask about their trip.

- I hope your trip from Montana has gone well.
- Did you run into a lot of traffic coming in from the airport?

- Have you been getting this much rain in Miami?
- How do you like Chicago?

Icebreaking discussions should take up no more than 2 or 3 minutes of the interview, as you and the candidate settle down. You can then move smoothly into explaining the interview process and giving the candidate a clear understanding of what will occur that day.

Behavior-Based Interview Questions

Here are hundreds of sample Behavior-Based Interview questions you can use as you prepare for your own interviews. They are divided into 50 different competency areas (refer to the end of this chapter for a full list) to make them easy to navigate and to help you choose the best questions for the competency areas you specifically want to assess.

Competency 1: Adaptability/Flexibility

- Describe a situation in which you had to adjust to a change over which you had no control.
- Sometimes we all have to work with people whose style differs from our own. Can you tell me about a time when you had to adjust to a colleague's work style to finish an important project?
- Have you ever taken on an assignment without knowing how you were going to do it? What happened?
- Tell me about a time when you had to think on your feet to extricate yourself from a difficult situation.
- Describe the most demanding manager you've ever worked for, and tell me how you adapted to his or her style.
- Sometimes we have jobs or projects that change in midstream. Tell me about a time when this happened to you and how you dealt with it.

Competency 2: Analysis

- Tell me about a time when you had to analyze information and make a decision.
- Tell me about an analytical project you took on that was not in your job description. Why did you do it?
- How do you use numbers to measure business performance? Give me an example.

- Describe one of your most difficult analyses. What made it difficult? Could you have done anything to make it easier? What was the result?
- What steps do you take to study a problem before making a decision? Use an example to illustrate this.
- Tell me about a time when you had to analyze something without existing guidelines or examples. How did you approach the problem? What were the results?

Competency 3: Assertiveness

- Give me an example where your self-confidence allowed you to take action when others might have avoided it. What was the result?
- Have you ever held back from doing something that you felt should be done? Why, and what happened as a result?
- Tell me about a time when you felt like a "fish out of water." What did you do to increase your comfort level?
- Describe a situation in which you had to give your manager some unwelcome news.
- Tell me about a time when you were assertive on someone else's behalf.
- Describe a recent experience when you were faced with poor service or unacceptable quality. What did you do about it? What was the result?

Competency 4: Attention to Detail

- Tell me about some times when you found errors in your work. What caused them? What did you do about them?
- Give me some examples of times when you knew things were not going well with a particular project, process, or activity. How did you know? What did you do to correct the problems?
- Tell me about a time when your attention to detail benefited your company.
- We've all experienced something "slipping through the cracks." Tell me about a time when this happened to you, what you did about it, and what, if anything, you did to prevent it from happening again.
- Describe a recent situation in which attention to detail was critical to success. How did you contribute?
- In many projects, it's essential to keep track of details while still managing the big picture. Tell me about a project where you did

this effectively. How did you make sure everything got done? How did you stay focused on the larger goal?

Competency 5: Collaboration

- How do you stay informed about what is happening in other departments of your company? Be specific.
- What do you do when you are faced with problems you can't solve within your unit or team? Share an example.
- Have you built a resource network outside your department? Tell me about a time when this network paid off for you and your company.
- Tell me about a time when you collaborated with someone who had a very different style from yours. Was this a problem or a bonus?
- Describe a situation in which you worked collaboratively with people at very different levels from yourself—either much higher, much lower, or both.
- Tell me about a project you worked on that involved people from many different areas of the company. What did you do to make that project successful?

Competency 6: Commitment to Task

- Tell me about a time when you overcame very difficult challenges to get a job done.
- In the last year, what project or initiative did you abandon? Why? How could you have saved it?
- When have you been a "champion" for something you considered important? What did that entail?
- We all become discouraged from time to time. Think about a recent situation when you felt discouraged about not being able to complete a task.
- Share a story about a project that dragged out much longer than anticipated. What did you do to be sure it was completed?
- What prevents you from completing tasks you've been assigned? Give me two specific examples.

Competency 7: Conflict Management

- Have you ever worked with someone you did not get along with? How did you handle the situation? What was the outcome?

- Describe a recent situation in which you have had to work with someone who clearly did not like you. How did that make you feel? What did you do about it?
- Tell me about a situation in which you successfully resolved a conflict with another person. What was the outcome?
- Can you tell me about a time when your actions had a negative effect on others?
- Tell me about a time when you resolved a conflict with a customer.
- *For managers:* How do you handle conflict among your staff members? Describe a recent situation you faced and how you dealt with it.

Competency 8: Control

- Tell me about the systems you use to keep track of tasks and important events. Give me an example of a time when these systems failed and how you dealt with it.
- What ideas have you come up with that have given you better information with which to make decisions? Be specific.
- How do you track your progress on a key project or long-range goal? Illustrate using a recent project.
- Share an example of a time when you had to document a sequence of events after the fact. How accurate were you?
- *For managers:* Walk me through your process for keeping track of what your direct reports are doing. Be specific.
- *For managers:* What process do you use to document your employees' performance? Give me an example of this process in action.

Competency 9: Creativity/Innovation

- In your last position, what good idea did you come up with that was implemented?
- Think about a time when someone brought you an idea that was odd or unusual. What did you do about it?
- Tell me about the most creative work-related project you have completed.
- Give me an example of a time when you came up with a cost-cutting idea.
- What do you do differently from others who have held your job? Why? How has this benefited your company? Be specific.

- Describe an innovative idea you developed that led to the success of a company initiative.
- Do you think of yourself as an "out-of-the-box" thinker? Can you give me a specific example of a creative solution that you came up with?
- What is the biggest contribution you have made to the profitability of a business?

Competency 10: Crisis Management

- Describe a recent time when your work was very hectic. What did you do to keep it under control? How many extra hours did you work? For how long?
- Crises usually require us to act quickly. In retrospect, how would you have handled a recent crisis differently, if you had been given more time to think before acting?
- Tell me about a crisis you could have prevented. Did you do anything differently after the crisis had passed?
- Tell me about a time when you had to deal with a crisis at work. What was the situation, and what did you do to mitigate it?
- *For managers:* Tell me how you resolve crises by deploying your team members. Give me a specific example.
- *For managers:* What do you do to keep team spirits up during a crisis situation? Give me a recent example.

Competency 11: Customer Focus/Customer Service Orientation

- Tell me about the most difficult customer situation you have ever handled. What did you do, and what was the outcome?
- What do you do when a customer is irate? Give me a specific example.
- Tell me about the last time a coworker asked you for help at a time when you were very busy with work of your own. What was the situation? What did you do?
- Describe a recent customer complaint that you handled. What was the complaint? How did you learn about it? How did it turn out?
- What lessons have you learned about keeping the customer satisfied? How did you learn them? Give me an example of how you learned one of these lessons.

- Can you think of a time when your loyalty was divided between the customer and the company? Tell me about it. What did you do?

Competency 12: Deadline Responsiveness

- Tell me about a time when you missed an important deadline. How could you have avoided this?
- How do you ensure that you keep projects on schedule and complete tasks on time? Describe your process, using a recent example.
- Give me an example of when you met an "impossible" deadline. How did that make you feel?
- Tell me about your most deadline-driven job, and give me some examples of deadlines you met and those you missed.
- What do you do when you are faced with an inflexible deadline and not enough time or resources to complete the task? Give me a specific example.
- When deadlines loom, sometimes something has to give. Tell me about a time when you compromised quality or skimped on a process to meet a deadline. How did you choose what to compromise? What was the outcome?

Competency 13: Dealing with Change

- What problems are you currently working on that came as a surprise to you?
- Tell me about a time when you were surprised by a change at work. How did you deal with it?
- What was your most challenging career transition? What did you do to make it successful?
- Walk me through the steps you took to acclimate yourself during the first week in your job at [company].
- Give me an example of a time when you responded quickly to a change. What was the situation? What was the outcome?
- Tell me about a time when you did not deal well with a change. What prevented you? What could you have done differently? What was the outcome?

Competency 14: Decision Making/Decisiveness/Judgment

- What is the most difficult business decision you have had to make? How did you arrive at your decision?

- Describe a situation in which you had to make a decision without having all the information you needed. How did you make this decision?
- We don't always have the luxury of time when making decisions. Can you give me an example of a decision you had to make in a hurry?
- Tell me about a complex decision that you made recently. How did you make the decision? What were the key elements you considered? What was the outcome?
- Tell me about the last time you made a decision when the instructions you were given were unclear, ambiguous, or contradictory. How did you decide what to do? What alternatives did you consider? How did the decision work out?
- Tell me about the kinds of decisions you make rapidly, and those you ponder longer. Share specific examples.
- Tell me about a decision you made that turned out badly. In hindsight, what would you have done differently?
- How do you balance instinct with facts when making decisions? Give me a specific example.
- Tell me about a time when you were forced to make an unpopular decision.
- *For managers:* Do you include your subordinates in your decision-making process? Give me an example in which their input was critical, and an example in which you overrode their recommendations.

Competency 15: Delegation

- Tell me about your biggest mistake in delegating. Why did you make this mistake?
- Give me an example of a time when you required help from your staff to deal with a major problem. How much authority did you delegate to them?
- Please discuss a time when you delegated a project effectively.
- Tell me about a time when you should have delegated but did not. What were the repercussions?
- Tell me about an instance when you delegated work to another person who didn't get the job done. Why did it happen? What did you do about it?
- How do you determine which staff members should handle which assignments? Illustrate with some examples.

Competency 16: Fact Finding

- Tell me about a time when you had to review detailed reports or documents to identify a problem.
- When you are given a new assignment, what is your procedure for gathering background information? Give me an example.
- Describe a situation that required you to interview several people to obtain some critical information. How did you know what to ask?
- Give an example that illustrates how you use fact-finding skills to gather information to solve a problem.
- Think of a time when the information you gathered was used to make a critical business decision. Was your information accurate and complete? How did the decision work out?
- Give me an example of a time when you made a poor decision because the facts you gathered were incorrect or incomplete.

Competency 17: Follow-up

- Tell me about the systems and processes that you use to ensure good follow-up. Walk me through the follow-up steps of a recent project.
- Describe a situation in which your follow-up was credited for capturing a business opportunity.
- We've all experienced times when we have forgotten to follow up. Tell me about one of those times. What did you learn from this that you used later? How did you use it?
- Tell me about some follow-up tasks that you have enjoyed and some that you have found difficult.

Competency 18: Goal Orientation/Goal Setting

- Tell me about a recent goal that you set and achieved. Walk me through your thinking and planning processes.
- Give an example of a goal that you did not reach. How did you feel about that? What could you have done differently?
- Describe a time when you set your sights too high.
- Describe a time when you set your sights too low.
- Tell me about an instance when you were unwilling to make the necessary sacrifice to achieve a goal.
- Think of a job you held where your goals were not clearly defined. What did you do about it?

Competency 19: Impact

- Describe a time when you inspired someone on your work team.
- Please tell me of an occasion when you were able to turn around the opinion of a group.
- Describe a time when you were nominated for a leadership role. Why do you think that happened? What was the outcome?
- With what groups or individuals do you have the greatest impact? Please share some examples.

Competency 20: Independence

- Tell me about some on-the-job rules or policies you didn't agree with. What did you do about it?
- What do you do in your job that isn't covered in your job description?
- Tell me about a situation in which you took matters into your own hands, even though it should have been handled by your manager. What was the outcome?
- Think about the boss who has given you the most independence. How did you respond? What problems did you encounter?
- Can you share an example of a situation in which you had to go against general feelings or policies to achieve a goal?
- In your current job, what constraints make it difficult to get things done? What do you do about them?

Competency 21: Initiative

- Sometimes opportunities come disguised as problems. Can you tell me about a time when you realized an opportunity? What did you do? What were the results?
- How did you get your job at [company]?
- Describe some ways in which you changed your job at [company]. What were the results?
- What do you do that is different from others in your profession? Give me an example of how that has worked out well for your employer.
- Tell me about a project that you initiated. What did you do? Why? What was the outcome?
- *For managers:* Describe some ways you have found to make your employees' jobs easier. What have been the benefits?

Competency 22: Integrity

- Think about a time when your integrity was challenged. How did you handle it?
- Tell me about a business situation in which you felt it was best not to be honest. What did you do?
- Describe a company policy that you conformed to but did not agree with. Why?
- Sometimes we all bend or stretch the truth just a bit—to succeed in something important, make a big sale, or avoid an unpleasant situation. Give me some examples of when you have done this. How did you feel about it?
- Tell me about a situation in which your manager asked you to do something that you didn't agree with. How did you handle this situation?
- Tell me about a time when you saw someone bend too far, when you questioned their integrity. What did you do?

Competency 23: Interpersonal Skills

- Give me a specific example of when you had to work with a difficult customer.
- Describe some situations in which you wished you'd acted differently with someone. What did you do? What happened?
- Tell me about a work situation that required you to adapt to a wide variety of people. What did you find difficult about that? What did you enjoy?
- Most of us have worked with people with whom we don't get along very well. How have you handled this in the past? Give me a specific example.
- *For managers:* What specific problems have members of your team brought to you recently? How did you handle them?
- *For managers:* All managers must deal with problem employees from time to time. Give me a recent example of when you had to deal with an employee who was causing a problem. What did you say? What did you do?

Competency 24: Leadership

- Describe a recent initiative that you led. What obstacles did you face in reaching your goals? How did you overcome them?

- Have you ever had difficulty getting others to accept your ideas? What was your approach? Did it work?
- Tell me about a situation in which you had to coordinate several people to achieve a goal. What prompted you to take the lead? How did you go about coordinating and leading the group? How did the group members respond to your leadership?
- Have you ever had to step in in midstream to rescue a project that was failing? What did you do, and what were the results? How did you gain the support of your team?
- Tell me about a situation in which you had to lead many people to achieve a goal.
- Share an experience in which you had to lead a technical team whose members had more expertise than you had. How did you deal with that?
- Describe a recent project you led that fell short of its goals. What were your obstacles? Why were they insurmountable? In retrospect, what would you have done differently?
- Tell me about a new policy or idea you implemented that was a considerable change from your standard procedures. What did you do to get people to go along with it?
- Describe a recent situation that illustrates your style in taking charge and leading others to achieve a goal.
- What are some of the most difficult one-on-one meetings you've had with employees? Why were they difficult? How could you have made them easier?
- Describe a group you led whose members didn't work well together. What did you do to improve teamwork?
- How do you communicate change to your group? Share some examples.
- Tell me about a time when you had to get an extra effort from your group. What did you do to motivate them? How did they respond?
- Have you ever had to fire an employee? What were the circumstances? How did you handle it?
- One of the most difficult leadership challenges is getting results from people over whom you have no direct authority. Can you give me any examples of how you've done that?

Competency 25: Learner Attitude

- Tell me about a recent situation that you would describe as a real learning experience. What did you learn? How have you applied it since then?
- Describe a decision you made that you would handle differently if you had to do it over again.
- What tricks or techniques have you learned to make a job easier? How did you learn them?
- Tell me about a recent training course you've taken. Why did you decide to take it? How has it helped you in your job? Give me a specific example.
- Think about a time when you had to learn new responsibilities. How did you learn them? How long did it take? What problems did you encounter?
- Give me some specific examples of different ways you've learned—in classroom settings, books, online, tele-training. Which did you find most effective? Why?

Competency 26: Listening

- We've all had times when we've misinterpreted something that someone told us. Give me an example of when this happened to you and what you did about it.
- Tell me about a time when your active listening skills really paid off for you—maybe a time when other people missed the key idea being expressed.
- Tell me about some of your assignments that required you to rely on oral information to get the job done. Did you have any problems with that?
- Tell me about a time when critical information had to be relayed in a hurry. What was the outcome?

Competency 27: Logic

- Tell me about a complex problem that you solved recently. How did you decide what to do? What were the key elements that you considered? What was the outcome?
- Give me an example of when you used instinct instead of logic to solve a problem. What was the result? How did you feel about it?

- Tell me about a time when your logical solution was overridden by someone senior at your company. How did that make you feel? What was the outcome?
- Describe your thought process when analyzing data to come to a decision. Share an example.

Competency 28: Negotiation

- Tell me about your most creative negotiation.
- Tell me about a time when you had to work hard to rescue a stalled negotiation. What did you do? What was the result?
- Give me an example of a time when you had to compromise to reach an agreement with someone. Did you feel the resolution was fair?
- Tell me about one of your negotiations that was unsuccessful. What was the fallout? What could you have done differently?
- What information do you gather before a negotiation, and how do you use this information during the negotiating process? Share some specific examples.
- What strengths do you bring to the negotiating table? Give me an example of how you have used these strengths during a negotiation.

Competency 29: Oral Communication

- Tell me about an instance in which you were unable to get your point across to someone on the telephone. How could you have avoided this problem?
- Tell me about a time when you had to be assertive to get across a point that was important to you.
- Give me an example of a time when you had to communicate bad news to someone.
- Describe a complex process, product, situation, or rule that you had to explain to someone. How did you know you were successful in getting your point across?
- Describe a time when you were able to gain support for an unpopular decision. What communications strategies did you use?
- Describe any formal or informal experience you have had in training someone else. How successful were you?

Competency 30: Persistence/Tenacity

- Have you ever been accused of giving up too soon? What was the situation?
- Tell me about a long-range goal that you achieved recently. How did you ensure that you were making progress over many weeks or months?
- Describe a situation in which you were able to reach a goal because you refused to give up. How long did you persist?
- What are some big obstacles that you've had to overcome in order to get where you are today? How did you overcome them?

Competency 31: Persuasiveness

- Relate an experience in which you were able to get others to follow your lead.
- How successful are you at getting people to do what you want them to do? What approach do you take? Give me two examples.
- What is the best idea you ever sold to your boss? What was your approach?
- Describe a situation in which you were able to convince someone to see things your way.
- Tell me about a time when you were unable to sell an idea or plan that you thought was the best approach. Why were you unsuccessful? What could you have done differently?
- Do you consider yourself a "natural salesperson"? Share some stories that illustrate this.
- Tell me about a time when you were able to turn someone's opinion completely around. How did you convince that person?

Competency 32: Planning and Organizing

- Give me a specific example of a project that you planned. How did you organize and schedule the tasks? Tell me about your action plan.
- Tell me about a time when you organized an event that was very successful.
- Give me an example of an event or project that you planned on very short notice.
- Recall a time when you were assigned a complex project. What steps did you take to prepare for and finish the project? Were you happy with the outcome? What one step would you have done differently?

- Describe a project you led that involved many team members. How did you make the best use of your resources?
- Tell me about a time when lack of organization caused you to miss an opportunity or a deadline. What did you do to prevent that from happening again?

Competency 33: Presentation

- Tell me about a recent successful experience making a speech or giving a presentation.
- When you are preparing and giving an oral presentation, how do you take your audience's needs into consideration? Give me an example.
- Have you ever been appointed spokesperson for a group? Tell me about it.
- Tell me about a time when you gave a presentation to a challenging audience. How did you deal with that audience? What was the outcome?

Competency 34: Priority Setting

- What do you do when you have too many tasks to accomplish in the time allowed? Give me a specific example.
- Describe a situation that required you to do a number of things at the same time. How did you handle it? What was the result?
- We have all faced short deadlines for important projects. How do you decide what to do first? Give me an example.
- How do you make sure that you are spending time on projects that are important but not necessarily urgent? Give me a recent example.

Competency 35: Problem Solving

- Tell me about the most perplexing problem you have faced in the last year.
- We can sometimes identify a small problem and fix it before it becomes a big problem. Give me an example of when you have done this.
- Describe a situation in which your manager was not available and a problem arose that needed immediate attention. How did you handle it?
- What is your typical way of dealing with conflict? Give me an example.

- Tell me about a time when you came up with a solution to a problem that others had not been able to solve for quite a while.
- In your last job, what problems did you identify that had previously been overlooked? What did you do about them?
- What kinds of problems do you deal with in your current job? How do you address them? Share some examples.
- Give me an example of a business problem you solved on your own, and one you solved with a group. How did your process differ?

Competency 36: Rapport Building

- How do you "break the ice" with clients? With coworkers? With subordinates? With your manager? Share some examples.
- Tell me about a time when you built rapport with a difficult customer.
- Describe a situation in which you were a new member of an existing group. How did you build rapport with your team members?
- Tell me about a business situation in which you found it difficult to establish rapport with someone. What was the outcome?

Competency 37: Resilience

- We all experience disappointments in life. Can you give me an example of how you coped with a work-related disappointment?
- Describe a recent situation that tested your coping skills.
- Tell me about an idea of yours that you could not implement. What happened, and how did that make you feel?
- What kinds of obstacles have you faced to get where you are today? How did you keep going when things didn't go your way? Give me some examples.

Competency 38: Resourcefulness

- Tell me about a problem that you've solved in an unusual way.
- How did you build your network of resources at your current job?
- Describe a situation in which you were blocked from reaching a goal. What did you do?
- Describe an instance in which you had to think on your feet to extricate yourself from a problem.
- What is the most unusual request you've received at work in the last year? How did you respond?

- Have you ever been given an assignment to do but not the resources to do it? How did you handle it? Give me a specific example.

Competency 39: Risk Taking

- Tell me about a risky move you made at work and why you made it.
- Describe a situation in which you made a decision without having all the necessary information. How did you decide?
- Describe a major transition in your career. What prompted you to make this change?
- Give me an example of a time when you decided not to take action, even though you were pressured to do so. How did you evaluate the situation? What was the result?

Competency 40: Sensitivity to Others

- When you are dealing with individuals or groups, how do you know when you are pushing too hard? What do you do about it? Share an example.
- Tell me about a time when a colleague was going through a rough time at work. How did you know? What actions did you take?
- Have you ever found it necessary to change your actions or behaviors to respond to the needs of another person? What was the situation?
- Discuss a time when you worked to understand a perspective different from your own. What was the outcome?

Competency 41: Staff Development

- *For managers:* Tell me about a person you managed who has advanced in his or her career. What role did you play?
- *For managers:* Tell me about the last person you hired who just didn't work out. What was the problem? How did you try to correct it? What was the outcome?
- *For managers:* Give me a specific example of how you have empowered your staff to make independent decisions.
- *For managers:* Describe a training program you implemented for your staff. How did you identify the need? How did you select the solution? What were the results?

- *For managers:* Tell me about a staff member who had a development need that you documented on his or her performance evaluation. What happened as a result? How did you help?
- *For managers:* Give an example of when you coached someone through a difficult situation. What did you advise? What was the outcome?

Competency 42: Strategic Planning

- Describe a situation in which you anticipated the future and made changes to current products to meet future customer needs.
- Describe a time when there were competitive threats in your marketplace and you developed actions to compete.
- Give me an example of when you identified and assessed a new business opportunity.
- How did you go about setting objectives for your group this year? Be specific.
- Have you ever recognized a problem before your manager or others in the organization recognized it? Tell me about it.
- Tell me about an idea or project you conceived recently. How did you know it was needed? How did you know it would work? What was the outcome?

Competency 43: Team Building

- Describe a situation in which you developed a group into a strong working team.
- Tell me about an instance in which you were able to build team spirit in a time of low morale.
- Tell me about the most challenging team project you have led. What did you do to ensure its success?
- Tell me some ways in which you have contributed to team effectiveness when you were not a designated team leader.

Competency 44: Teamwork

- Tell me about the most successful team you have ever been on. What made it work?
- Describe a time when team members had to arrive at a compromise to get the job done. What was your role in making that happen?

- Tell me about a specific time when a team member wasn't contributing to a project you were working on. What was the situation, and what steps did you take to resolve the problem? What was the outcome?
- Tell me about a time when your team did not agree with your ideas. How did you deal with the situation?
- Not all teams are compatible. Think of a team you worked with whose members didn't get along. What happened?
- How have you handled conflict or criticism within a team you've been on? What was the outcome?

Competency 45: Technical and Professional Knowledge and Proficiency

In addition to the general competency questions included here, you will need to develop customized questions to assess the professional/technical knowledge and skills required for the position at hand. For example, for a manufacturing worker, you will need to find out about equipment operation skills and safety awareness. For a public relations executive, you might want to assess media relations skills. A programmer must be competent in the specific languages and systems used by your company. In addition to Behavior-Based questions, you will want to include in your Interview Guide a series of traditional and situational questions to gather this information; examples are included later in this chapter.

- Sometimes it is easy to get in over your head. Tell me about a time when you had to request help or assistance for a project or assignment that was beyond your capability.
- Give me an example of how you applied your existing knowledge to a new assignment.
- Tell me about a time when you were called in as the technical expert for a project. What value did you bring? How did the project turn out?
- Give me an example of how you acquired a technical skill and converted it into a practical application.

Competency 46: Time Management

- What do you do when your time schedule is disrupted by unforeseen circumstances? Share a specific example.
- How do you manage your schedule so that you have time for important projects as well as day-to-day responsibilities? Please share a specific example.

- What prevents you from completing daily tasks? Walk me through a recent day on the job.
- Tell me about a time when you had to work overtime or extra hours to get an important job done. In retrospect, what could you have done differently to reduce your overtime hours?

Competency 47: Tolerance for Stress

- How do you deal with pressure in your job? Give me specific examples.
- Tell me about an unexpectedly stressful situation you experienced at work. How did you handle it?
- Have you ever had a feeling of frustration and impatience when dealing with a customer? What was the situation?
- Give me some examples of when your ideas were strongly opposed in a meeting. How did you react?
- What are the highest-pressure situations that you've faced in recent years? How did you cope?
- Think of your most productive work experience. What stress levels were you under? Did that add to or hinder your productivity?

Competency 48: Versatility

- Tell me about a time when you were required to "wear many hats."
- Describe a time when you were working on several projects at once. How did you make the transition from one to the next over the course of a day?
- Tell me about a time when your manager called on you to take on a special project outside your usual area of activity. Why were you selected? What was the outcome?
- Share a situation in which you were required to change the way you normally work and found it difficult to do so.

Competency 49: Work Standards

- Tell me about a time when you were required to turn in what you felt was not your best work. What was the situation? How did it make you feel?
- Give me two examples of things you've done in previous jobs that show your willingness to work hard.
- Have you disagreed with a manager's evaluation of your performance? How did you handle the situation?

- Share an example of when you weren't very pleased with your work performance. What did you do about it?
- In your current position, how do you define doing a good job? Give me some examples of when your definition was not met and what you did about it.
- Describe a time when your results did not meet your manager's expectations. What happened? What action did you take?
- Consider times when you did your best work and other times when you didn't. Give me an example of each time. What made the difference?
- *For managers:* How do you judge the performance of your employees? What distinguishes "good" from "average"? Tell me about an employee you evaluated as "average" and how you helped him or her to become "good."

Competency 50: Written Communication

- Tell me about a time when you used your written communication skills to get an important point across.
- Describe a difficult writing challenge. Could you have done something different to make it easier?
- Describe a report or proposal that you wrote that was very effective. How did you know? What was the outcome?
- Tell me about a time when you used written communication to turn around someone's opinion. Did you enjoy the challenge?
- Tell me about some of the typical written assignments in your last position. Which ones were most challenging? Which did you enjoy most? Give me specific examples.
- Describe the most significant written document that you have had to complete. What was riding on it?

Behavior-Based Interview Questions for Job and Company Fit or for Motivation

Not every individual who qualifies for a job is a good fit for the job or the company. The following questions will help you assess whether an individual will perform well within the specific structure of the job and the culture of the company. There are no "right" or "wrong" answers to these questions, but you need to keep in mind what will be expected of the individual holding the job. For example, the first question asks about a structured versus an unstructured environment. If the position is in a highly structured department or would report to a highly structured boss, someone who thrives best in an unstructured environment might be constantly chafing against the environment of the job or become unproductive within its confines. The third question delves into what makes an individual look forward to going to work every day. When you ask this question, assess the response against the structure, environment, mission, and culture of the specific job and of the company to see if this candidate will be motivated and energetic. The seventh question, "Why did you choose this type of work?" might reveal insights into a person's motivations and passions that can be very valuable in assessing fit.

These job- or company-fit questions are especially helpful when you have narrowed down your slate of candidates to a handful of qualified individuals. All of them have the skills, knowledge, and performance traits that will enable them to be successful. Yet there will be subtle or not-so-subtle differences in what motivates, energizes, and stimulates them on the job. Tie the answers you get to the job-related competencies that are critical for your open position and to the opportunities available in the job and at your company. These questions will help you assess their differences so you can make the best choice for your specific opening.

- Give me an example of when you had to deal with an unstructured environment in which there was a lot of change.
- Give me an example of when you went above and beyond the call of duty.
- When did you love what you were doing? Give me a specific example.
- When did you hate what you were doing? Describe the situation.
- What gave you the greatest feeling of achievement in your job at [company]? Why was this so satisfying?
- Describe the time when you worked the hardest and felt the greatest sense of achievement.
- Why did you choose this type of work?
- Give me some examples of activities in your last job that were satisfying and some that were less satisfying.

> **TIP:** As we mentioned in Chapter 3, you can add a motivational component to almost any Behavior-Based Interview question. Simply follow up the response by asking, "How satisfied/dissatisfied were you with that?" and you will gain insight into the unique motivators for that candidate.

- All jobs have their difficulties and frustrations. Tell me some specific tasks or assignments that you found dissatisfying. Why were you dissatisfied, and what did you do about it?
- Can you tell me about a time when you took on responsibilities outside your job description? Why did you do that?
- What people or events have been the most important in your professional development?
- What have you done in your last job that makes you feel most proud?
- Tell me about the last time you became frustrated at work.
- Tell me about a particularly boring or distasteful task you have faced in the last year or so. What made it boring or distasteful? What did you do to ensure that the task was accomplished?
- What did you like best about your job at [company]?
- What were your reasons for leaving?
- Tell me about some recent responsibilities you have taken on. Was this your own idea?
- Tell me about a performance evaluation that pointed out a development need. How did your manager present this to you? How did that make you feel? What did you do about it, and what was the result?
- Tell me about the most difficult group of people you've worked with.
- Tell me about the best boss you've had. Be specific.
- What motivates you to work hard? Give me some examples.

Follow-up Questions (Probes)

Candidates don't always provide a complete SAR story in their response. Because you need to document the entire situation, action, and result to assess the candidate fairly on that particular competency, you will need to use probing questions to draw out additional details and prompt a complete SAR response. You can add to your toolkit these sample probing questions:

- And then what happened?
- Can you tell me more about . . . ?
- Did you feel well prepared for that? What did you do to prepare?
- Do you wish you had done something differently? Please explain.
- Give me another example.
- How did it turn out?
- How did they respond?
- How did you feel about that?
- How did you get involved?
- How did you make that happen?
- How did you prepare for that?
- How did you resolve that?
- How did your team react?
- Lead me through your thought process.
- That sounds difficult. Tell me more about how you did it.
- Tell me more about . . .
- Tell me more about the obstacles you were facing.
- Was that difficult for you?
- Was your manager pleased?
- Were you happy with that result?
- What actions did you take?
- What did you do next?
- What did you learn from that?
- What did the other person say?
- What did you say?
- What do you wish you had done differently?
- What happened next?
- What obstacles did you face? How did you overcome them?
- What was most difficult about that?
- What was the outcome?
- What was your reaction?
- What was your reasoning?
- What was your role?
- What were you thinking at that point?
- When did that occur?
- Who else was involved?
- Why did you decide to do that?
- Why did you take that action?

Put Candidates at Ease

Because Behavior-Based Interviewing is a structured process, interviewers are well prepared. Armed with their Interview Guides, they are ready to move through their preselected questions and probes and take notes on each candidate's SARs. Especially for those new to Behavior-Based Interviewing, this structure and preparation might lead them to present a somewhat "clinical" appearance to candidates. Candidates might feel there is little give-and-take, that they are simply responding to questions without getting a reaction or response from the interviewer. This can be an off-putting experience.

When interviewing, try to pose your questions in a natural manner, and don't be afraid to inject your own natural reaction to a candidate's responses. "Wow, that sounds interesting." "I know what you mean, I really love a challenge, too." "You're right, the industry has undergone some dramatic changes." Even your probes and follow-up questions can relate back to something the candidate said, to promote the feeling of dialogue rather than interrogation. For example, "What an up-and-down experience! You said customers really liked the change. How do you know that? Did you track customer satisfaction scores?"

Always remember that the vast majority of candidates are nervous and keyed up. They want to make a great impression, and they want to establish rapport as well as answer questions. A smile, a warm manner, and visible responsiveness to their comments will help put them at ease. Don't get so wrapped up in asking questions and noting answers that you appear more a researcher than an interviewer.

Traditional and Situational Questions

As discussed extensively in the first three chapters of this book, traditional and situational interview questions do not provide interviewers with specific examples of a candidate's past behaviors. Rather, they allow the candidate to provide general information that he might or might not be able to support with a complete SAR. In addition, these types of questions might lead the candidate to provide information that she thinks the interviewer wants to hear. For example, if you asked a candidate interviewing for an accounting position, "What are your greatest strengths?" you might hear, "I have a natural affinity for numbers and I really understand how financial results relate to business success. I am very detail oriented, and I have excellent tracking and follow-up skills, so that nothing slips through the cracks." Good answer! Of course, you will want to probe further and gather evidence of those strengths in the form of SAR responses to Behavior-Based Interview questions. But traditional and situational questions can be very helpful in gathering information about credentials, educational qualifications, previous work environments, and job-related knowledge, and they can be a good way to build rapport before easing into Behavior-Based Interview questions.

In this section we provide sample *traditional* and *situational* questions that you might want to use as an initial screening tool or during the early stages of an interview. Then you can make the transition to Behavior-Based Interview questions to gather specific examples of when, where, how, and how successfully the specific skills were used.

Traditional Interview Questions

These questions will help you screen out a candidate who does not possess the essential competencies for the job. In many cases you can use these as a lead-in to a related Behavior-Based Interview question. For example, a very popular traditional interview question is, "What are your greatest strengths?" You can follow up the candidate's response with a question that zeroes in on one of the key competencies for the position: "Tell me about a time when your attention to detail benefited your company."

- Tell me about yourself. *(Note that this question is also listed in the beginning of this chapter as an icebreaker. It is a common way to begin an interview and might help to set a candidate at ease.)*
- What are your greatest strengths?
- What are your greatest weaknesses?
- Where do you want to be in five years?
- Why do you want to work for us?
- What is your experience with [competency, skill, function, etc.]?
- Do you work well under pressure?
- Do you consider yourself a leader or a follower?
- Do you work well with teams?
- Do you prefer a structured or a loose working environment?
- Are you a risk taker?
- What will your colleagues say about you?
- How will your subordinates describe you?
- What is the greatest value you bring to your organization?
- Define your leadership and management style.

- Describe your decision-making style.
- How do you determine or evaluate success?
- What are your views on continuing education? For yourself? For your employees?
- What have you been doing with your time since you left your last position?
- What have you done to improve your professional skills this year?
- What are you looking for in a new opportunity?
- What will you bring to this position that another candidate will not?
- How long do you expect to stay with our company?
- What are your compensation requirements?

Situational Interview Questions

Situational questions present hypothetical circumstances and give the candidate an opportunity to describe an "ideal" situation or how he "would" or "might" deal with a circumstance. These questions can be a good tool for gaining insight into a candidate's thought processes, but the information gleaned must not be taken at face value—it must be validated with SARs that are prompted through Behavior-Based Interview questions. Good follow-up questions are those related to job fit, company fit, and motivations. For example, after asking, "How would you describe your ideal boss?" you can follow up with a job-fit question: "Tell me about the best boss you've had. Give me some specific examples of why he or she was so great to work for."

- How would you describe your ideal position?
- How would you describe your ideal boss?
- When you are hiring, what do you look for as the most important attribute in a candidate?
- If you could change something about your career, what would it be and why?
- What type of person would you hire for this position?
- If we were to hire you, what would be the first thing you would do?
- What would you do if you had an employee who was consistently late for work?
- What would you do if a team member was not contributing to a project you were working on?
- What would you do in your first week on the job to ensure your long-term success with our company?

- How would you handle an irate customer?
- How would you deal with a communication problem at work?
- What would you do if you disagreed with a company policy?
- What would you do if your boss asked you to do something that you considered unethical?
- What would you do if your boss asked you to do something that was outside your job description?
- What would you do if you were asked to take on a new responsibility that you didn't feel prepared to handle?
- How do you deal with stress on the job?
- How would you handle a staff member's personal crisis that affected his or her work performance?
- Suppose we were to offer you the position of [job title]. If you could have only two other people working with you to meet the job challenges, what would those individuals be responsible for, and why?

Put It All Together

The questions in this chapter are a rich resource for your interview preparation. Not only will you find many specific Behavior-Based Interview questions that you can use exactly as written, but simply by reviewing the questions, you will gain a deeper understanding of how to phrase any additional questions you might need. The end result is that candidates will give you concrete, specific answers that are essential to accurately assessing their knowledge, skills, and motivators.

Integrated into the five-step process detailed in Chapter 3, these questions are the core of a successful Behavior-Based Interview program.

50 Competency Areas

1. Adaptability/Flexibility
2. Analysis
3. Assertiveness
4. Attention to Detail
5. Collaboration
6. Commitment to Task
7. Conflict Management
8. Control
9. Creativity/Innovation
10. Crisis Management

11. Customer Focus/Customer Service Orientation
12. Deadline Responsiveness
13. Dealing with Change
14. Decision Making/Decisiveness/Judgment
15. Delegation
16. Fact Finding
17. Follow up
18. Goal Orientation/Goal Setting
19. Impact
20. Independence
21. Initiative
22. Integrity
23. Interpersonal Skills
24. Leadership
25. Learner Attitude
26. Listening
27. Logic
28. Negotiation
29. Oral Communication
30. Persistence/Tenacity
31. Persuasiveness
32. Planning and Organizing
33. Presentation
34. Priority Setting
35. Problem Solving
36. Rapport Building
37. Resilience
38. Resourcefulness
39. Risk Taking
40. Sensitivity to Others
41. Staff Development
42. Strategic Planning
43. Team Building
44. Teamwork
45. Technical and Professional Knowledge and Proficiency
46. Time Management
47. Tolerance for Stress
48. Versatility
49. Work Standards
50. Written Communication

CHAPTER

5

Six Companies That Successfully Use Behavior-Based Interviewing

The measure of success is not whether you have a tough problem to deal with, but whether it is the same problem you had last year.
—John Foster Dulles

IN THIS CHAPTER we go from theory to proof. You will read profiles of six companies that have implemented Behavior-Based Interviewing and found that it delivered the following positive results: better hires, stronger retention, greater employee satisfaction, and increased customer satisfaction.

As you read these profiles, you will notice some interesting differences. The companies vary in size: TD Madison and Associates has fewer than 10 employees in one location, Randstad North America has 500 branch offices across the United States and Canada, and GE employs more than 300,000 people in 100 countries around the world. Their products and services are diverse: Hallmark Cards is in the "personal expressions" industry, Golden Corral is a nationwide restaurant chain, and InterContinental Hotels Group is a major player in the global hospitality industry. As you might imagine, their hiring needs cover the spectrum from front-line food-service staff to aircraft engineers and graphic designers to senior executives. In fact, you might think that these companies have very little in common.

Yet they all share a serious commitment to Behavior-Based Interviewing as the valuable methodology that enables them to choose the right person for the right job—every time.

In these profiles, you will read how and why the decision was made to introduce Behavior-Based Interviewing—what problems or challenges the companies faced, and how the new methods provided the solution. You'll read about potential pitfalls and how the program leaders and champions ensured companywide implementation. Most of all, what we hope you'll take away from these stories is an appreciation for the practical usefulness and tremendous value of Behavior-Based Interviewing. It works for Golden Corral, Randstad North America, InterContinental Hotels Group, TD Madison and Associates, Hallmark, and GE. It will work for your company, too.

Golden Corral

Lance Trenary, senior vice president of operations at Golden Corral, has two things in common with Elvis Presley: Both were born in Tupelo, Mississippi, and both started their careers by the age of 10. Elvis had his singing debut at age 10 in a youth talent contest at the Mississippi-Alabama Fair and Dairy Show; Lance started in the restaurant business when he was 6 years old. His family owned and operated 14 Pizza Hut franchises in Mississippi and Alabama where he helped out on weekends.

Lance has spent the last 18 years of his restaurant career at Golden Corral, the darling of the buffet restaurant business, where a top priority is hiring extraordinary people and matching the right talent with the right job and the company's unique culture. Golden Corral is a 30-year-old company with 125 company restaurants and 360 franchise restaurants across 41 states; a new restaurant opens every 10 days. In 2003 it reached a new milestone—over $1.2 billion in sales—and it is again on track to have its best year ever. To top it off, Ted Fowler, president and CEO, was named the 2003 Foodservice Operator of the Year and Gold Plate recipient, the highest possible recognition in the hospitality industry. Golden Corral continues to have remarkable performance even in turbulent economic times. So what's the secret?

Golden Corral makes *people* its top business priority. It is committed to finding and hiring extraordinary talent and then retaining and recognizing these employees. These are not just words on a sheet of paper tucked away in some manager's manual, but a way of life that is taken very seriously. The quality of the people gets top attention at every executive business review. Vice presidents present their "quality hire reports"— employee scorecards—as the first item on the agenda, even before sales and profit results are discussed. Golden Corral also re-implemented Behavior-Based Interviewing 36 months ago, and it has already seen amazing results. A turnover rate of nearly 60 percent for general managers has been reduced to single digits with cost savings of over $3 million. A turnover rate below 10 percent is unheard of in the restaurant business.

Golden Corral sets the bar high. It won't tolerate marginal performance, so it has developed a hiring and Behavior-Based Interviewing process that eliminates marginal candidates. A critical part of this process is a scoring system that rates candidates on the most important success indicators for their operations. A point value is assigned to such items as past experience, positions held, restaurant volume background, education level, and, most importantly, how candidates score on the Behavior-Based Interview itself. According to Lance, "We may have missed some really great people, but we had to draw the line somewhere and insist that we do not hire anyone below this level. This puts the odds in our favor for eliminating the risk of hiring a marginal person."

Judy Irwin, vice president of human resources and training, says that it's difficult for a candidate to misrepresent things during a Behavior-Based Interview. For example, one of the company's key competencies is customer service, so managers might ask a question such as, "Tell me about a time when you went out of your way to exceed a customer's expectations," with a series of follow-up questions such as, "Where were you working?" "Tell me about the specific circumstances," "Who was there?" and "Who can we talk to to verify that?" Judy says that Behavior-Based Interviews yield very reliable information because people can't help but be honest when they relate a specific situation. She says, "When you say, for example, tell me about a time when you had trouble coming to work on time, the stories people share are honest, and what they say can help you evaluate if this person is a good fit for the company culture or not. It's great finding out this information up front."

Before implementing Behavior-Based Interviewing, Lance and his team sought input from the company's best managers by holding a general manager roundtable; during this meeting they also gained buy-in and support for the implementation. They began the implementation by having an outside consulting firm study the top performers and best workers from each restaurant to come up with high-performance competencies and interview questions to ensure that they would hire top-performing restaurant workers and management teams. A pilot program was rolled out to 10 restaurants, and the results were tracked by assessing turnover rates, productivity rates, and employee satisfaction surveys. There were major improvements in all three categories even early in the process. A rollout program for the rest of the restaurants was then developed and launched.

To ensure companywide adoption and ongoing success of the program, regional meetings are held and managers receive training on how to administer Behavior-Based Interviews. There is a strong commitment to training every manager in the system because, with up to 80 workers in each restaurant, one manager alone can't handle all the interviewing. Every year Golden Corral holds a recertification process to refresh the learning and recommit the buy-in for using the system. Newly hired managers are required to go through a certification process during their initial 12-week training course.

Lance points out that it's important that interviews be customized for an organization. "What makes a successful Golden Corral general manager might not be what makes a successful general manager for another restaurant. Our culture is defined, and our requirements are very specific." Golden Corral has a distinct set of beliefs and values. One of those values is a strong work ethic. While its competitors look at Monday through Friday workweeks for their employees, Golden Corral doesn't find this effective because 65 percent of its business takes place on Friday and Saturday nights and on Sunday. Golden Corral believes it's important that its employees be there when the rest of the country is eating out. Of course it's made some accommodations for its employees, but working Friday, Saturday, and Sunday is required. Golden Corral is a performance-based organization, and employees have to perform if they are to stay around long term. It is also a company that constantly changes its business to meet the needs of guests. So hiring employees who can handle a lot of change, work in a performance-based environment, and have a strong work ethic is what makes Golden Corral successful.

Behavior-Based Interviewing allows Golden Corral hiring managers to look at what drives candidates to be successful—to get to the inner person—in addition to evaluating technical competencies so that they can match the right people with their open positions. Golden Corral also uses Behavior-Based Interviewing for all internal promotions. Lance shared an example of why this is important. At one point, before Behavior-Based Interviewing was implemented, an individual was promoted to a higher-level management position because he expressed an interest and because he was a great general manager. But he was not successful in his new role, and he ended up leaving the company. This situation would have been avoided if Behavior-Based Interviewing had been used.

To ensure that every manager is utilizing Behavior-Based Interviewing, Golden Corral requires all managers to participate in training, and information is consistently communicated in newsletters, at conventions, and through train-the-trainer meetings. Currently, restaurant audits are performed and Interview Guides and forms are reviewed during the audit on every new hire. In the near future, Golden Corral will install a satellite system that will give the audit team the ability to see real-time Interview Guides and forms. If a restaurant hires 50 new people, the audit team will be able to see that 50 Behavior-Based Interviews were conducted. Using Behavior-Based Interviewing is nonnegotiable and is critical to the successful operations of Golden Corral.

Randstad North America

Randstad North America is in the business of hiring top-quality people for its clients. The company provides staffing solutions for clerical, industrial, technical, creative, and professional positions in all industries. In 2002 the company's branches placed over 200,000 people in more than 27,000 companies across the United States and Canada. You can bet Randstad takes hiring and interviewing practices seriously! Making the perfect match is the service it is providing.

Randstad North America has over 500 branches across the United States and Canada, 2500 employees on staff, and up to 50,000 outside talent filling flexible and permanent positions. At the heart of the company's branches are 1000 agents who are responsible for selling staffing solutions, building client relationships, and servicing client accounts. These agents also recruit, interview, coach, develop, and place talent. In this model, the agents really understand the needs of their clients so that they can provide the right talent and a good fit. Behavior-Based Interviewing enables agents to better market their outside talent to their clients. According to Joanne DeLavan Reichardt, vice president of public relations, "On a talent marketing call, it works better to say, 'I have a great talent with x skills, and let me tell you how she applied them in her last position' than it does to simply say, 'I have a great talent with x skills.' "

Gail Auerbach, managing director of human resources, believes that the best way to perform an effective candidate assessment is to use Behavior-Based Interviewing. To provide the best service possible for its clients, Randstad North America implemented Behavior-Based Interviewing in its business model in 1999 as part of the agent new-hire orientation. Once hired, agents are required to go through several weeks of rigorous training that exposes them to the corporate culture and way of doing business. The classes are intentionally small—only 12 people. Agents go through an entire section of training on Behavior-Based Interviewing, with role-playing and practice as part of the agenda. Follow-up continues after training, as the trainer provides a written report and also talks to each agent's manager about what needs to be reinforced. Six months later another follow-up call is made to the agent and his or her manager to make sure everything is being applied correctly.

During the initial orientation training sessions, agents are introduced to their computer tools, including a section that assists them with their candidate interviews. Prewritten Behavior-Based questions are built into the online system. Agents log into the system, enter the position they are trying to fill, and find a whole set of questions designed to fit that job. More than 1,000 agents across the United States and Canada share this very comprehensive database of questions, allowing them to assess talent in a similar manner. Agents are able to choose questions from the database and type candidate responses directly into the computer. "By using Behavior-Based Interviewing, Randstad North America makes matches based not only on the talent's skill level but also on work environment, ensuring that the talent has the competencies, such as customer-service orientation and teamwork, that are required by the client," says Joanne.

Because Behavior-Based Interviewing has been so successful in evaluating candidates for clients, Randstad is currently rolling out the process for its internal job openings. It developed a standardized set of competencies for three different position levels—managing directors, corporate directors, and field and staff. There are five groups of competencies, and interview questions tied to those competencies have been developed. About 95 percent of Randstad's openings are agent positions.

Gail and her team understand the importance of measuring and tracking quantifiable data. She is working to refine the assessment of a successful agent by creating a new profile after compiling a year's worth of data. This will allow Randstad to see which individuals have been successful agents and base the new hiring profile on proven success in the job. The company will look at quantitative data such as real sales results, retention rates, profit margins, and revenue goal achievement. "We think we know what makes a successful agent, but we're just scratching the surface. There are lots of different opinions, and now we have the opportunity to really find out what makes them successful. We will be able to determine if we need someone with proven sales, service, and/or human resources skills to fill those slots," says Gail.

Randstad's agents are making better hiring decisions, and they are presenting the best candidates to meet their clients' needs. By implementing Behavior-Based Interviewing internally, Randstad hopes to improve the caliber of the people it brings in, better understand how to develop its people, and get the right people in the right spots. Behavior-Based Interviewing works for Randstad because it's easy to use and agents don't have to think about it much. They just have to sign on to the computer, pick the questions they want to ask, and enter their notes. The system makes their lives easier and gives them the confidence of knowing that they are presenting high-quality candidates to their clients.

InterContinental Hotels Group

After many years of consolidations, mergers, acquisitions, and name changes, the new management team at InterContinental Hotels Group is injecting a new vitality and a refreshing way of doing business into this venerable organization, which traces its roots back to 1777. Along with this new vitality is a renewed focus on people and on ensuring that the right people are in the right roles. This priority comes straight from

Richard North, chief executive. There is a new openness from top management on down. There are no secrets, and along with that comes open communication about business changes and the reasons for them.

Tom Ruby, InterContinental Hotels Group's manager of curriculum & certification for the Americas, has implemented Behavior-Based Interviewing since the mid-1980s, and he is a big proponent of the techniques himself. That is because of his own success rate in hiring people. He's proud to say that a very high percentage of all the people he has personally hired over the last four decades are still employed at the company, have risen through the ranks, and have always performed at top levels.

InterContinental Hotels Group has more than 3300 hotels across 100 countries and territories and employs 31,000 people. In the 1980s Tom Ruby included Behavior-Based Interviewing in the hotel's general manager training curriculum. The company recognized that turnover of line management and staff—more than 30 percent—was a tremendous issue and that targeted measures had to be taken. Behavior-Based Interview training was piloted and received high ratings from the managers who participated. The system was then fully implemented and became part of the overall curriculum. Tom and his team took the program internationally to managers in Asia, Europe, the Middle East, and Africa. He specifically remembers instructing 60 managers in China through interpreters. They had never received this type of training before, and he could see them become animated and intrigued with the new interviewing techniques they were learning. There was tremendous acceptance of Behavior-Based Interviewing in every country, and it is an applicable skill that can be learned across a wide variety of cultures.

In the 1980s general managers in the United States were required to go through what was called "Phase A" and "Phase B" training to receive a certification of completion from what was then Holiday Inns. The certification was a distinguished achievement that was highly regarded in the industry.

Phase A training consisted of a two-week class covering topics such as a company overview, marketing, the Holidex reservation system, guest relations, and business and technical skills relevant to the job. The instruction was tailored around the managers' completing a hotel business and marketing plan. Managers were then sent home for six months to participate in the "application phase." They had to complete their business plans along with other leadership-related assignments. Phase B training followed the six-month application phase. The managers were brought back for another two weeks of training that included reviews of their application-phase assignments plus lessons on Behavior-Based Interviewing, situational leadership, conflict management, communications, and change management.

Over the years, the training structure in the United States and Canada evolved from a formalized process involving two 2-week sessions to a continuous learning environment. There is still an initial formalized and centralized management training segment, but now managers earn credits by attending ongoing workshops after their initial certification. Tom reexamined the management training program and included Behavior-Based Interviewing as a workshop option because of its importance. He says that this workshop has become one of the most popular with managers. Those on staff who teach Behavior-Based Interviewing have been certified by an outside consulting firm, and they are the experts and resources for the managers.

Tom has performed due diligence to see how the program is working. A month after their return from a training program, he has interviewed managers to find out what stood out, what needs improvement, and what skills they have already put to the test. He kept hearing over and over, "I had to hire someone as soon as I got back. Because our turnover has been so high, the Behavior-Based Interviewing skills helped me differentiate and recognize the better candidates. I now have the ability to ask better questions, I'm prepared and not just a résumé interviewer anymore, and I feel better about my ability to make hiring decisions." Overall, there seems to be a noticeable decrease in staff turnover whenever a general manager begins using Behavior-Based Interviewing.

Tom also made certain that managers got practice in interviewing and constructive feedback during their training sessions. To do this, he had participants work in small groups that included an interviewer, an interviewee, and a note taker as well as a facilitator. One of his trainers took a unique approach and invited college and even high school students to watch and participate. Managers were spellbound by their newfound ability to ask questions that would get stories from a candidate's past history book, rather than asking "what if" questions and getting hypothetical answers.

InterContinental Hotels Group takes very seriously the concept of hiring the best people using Behavior-Based Interviewing. In fact, it's a technique that can be used for every job level, even for hotel dishwashers. Tom says, "You need to see into a candidate's past and find out if they've been timely and how much they care about their work environment. Asking questions around how often they clean their car and change their oil helps you find out things that are relevant to the job. They will use the same or similar behaviors at work that they use at home and at school. The way they take care of their car will give you some insight on how they'll treat your ten-thousand-dollar dishwashing machine." He believes that successful organizations surround themselves with successful people, from the top down. The key is whom you hire, because you become whom you surround yourself with.

TD Madison and Associates

TD Madison and Associates, a top U.S. retained executive search firm located in Virginia, uses Behavior-Based Interviewing for assessing candidates; as a result, it has an extraordinarily high rate of placements—over 83 percent—and its clients keep coming back! Prior to using Behavior-Based Interviewing, there were times when they were unable to close the search. Why? Their clients would say, "Keep sending me candidates. I'll know it when I see it." This posed problems, especially when entire boards were involved in the hiring decision. According to Dean Madison, president of the firm, "There would always be one person versus someone else when making a decision, and decisions would be changed at the eleventh hour." Dean implemented Behavior-Based Interviews to better serve his clients and to give them more predictable outcomes with a more predictable hire. "We have an attitude that our clients are number one and if they are successful, we will be successful." As proof of its commitment to selecting the right-fit candidates who will improve retention rates and reduce the associated costs of employee turnover, the firm even teaches its clients how to implement this process for themselves. TD Madison and Associates' practices prove that the firm is more concerned about finding quality candidates—employees who it knows will be with its clients for a long time—rather than just making the deal.

What's unique about TD Madison and Associates is that it also uses the Behavior-Based questioning format when checking a potential hire's references. Answers received from these references either support or don't support earlier findings. Dean sees challenges in the traditional reference-checking process, as references are reluctant to say something negative about the candidate: "If you use the Behavior-Based approach and ask them to talk about how the candidate handled specific situations in the past, you get better-quality information. It's natural to talk about the situation, actions, and results, and you're not violating a person's confidence." For example, if integrity is a big issue, a question asked of a reference might be, "Tell me about a time when Bob was faced with a unique integrity challenge. What did he do?" The information obtained is fact-based and very helpful when TD Madison and Associates and its clients make their hiring decisions.

For each of his clients, Dean developed a skill-set analysis and a list of key competencies that reflect the unique culture of the company. These competencies are the benchmark for assessing candidates.

TD Madison and Associates gains many benefits from using Behavior-Based Interviewing, including the following:

- The firm learns more about a candidate in a few hours than it did using the traditional system, where it could spend all day interviewing a candidate and still not get all the facts.
- Behavior-Based Interviewing provides the firm with a better way to explain candidates' qualifications to clients. It no longer has to say that it has a "gut feeling" about someone.
- The system bridges the gap between company culture and skill requirements of the job.
- It provides line managers with a better pool of candidates who are the right fit.
- It allows them to communicate more universally with client CFOs and CTOs, for example, so that they don't talk just in terms of their trade.
- The firm provides data points and evaluations of candidates, rather than assumptions, and it submits only the best candidates.
- And, as we said, the firm gets great results in placements—over 83 percent—and its clients keep coming back because of the great matches.

Dean says that the firm is successful because "we have an imperative to give hiring managers credible information about candidates to make their hiring decisions. Their time is valuable, they have a task to do, but when it comes to hiring, they're going to make a decision whether they have the information or not. We enable them to make an educated decision." Dean also believes that line managers need to be held accountable for employee turnover as well as productivity. "Today you need high-end producers because there are only so many seats at the company and so many hours in the day, and you must maximize that. As we move forward with recovery, it's more important to properly analyze and assess candidates up front rather than throwing darts." TD Madison and Associates feels good about what it does because it finds the right person for the right opportunity and ensures the right selection. "There's no longer a place for traditional interviews in today's environment," says Dean.

Hallmark Cards, Inc.*

Despite its $4 billion in revenue and 20,000 employees throughout North America, the culture at Hallmark Cards remains a reflection of its private family ownership and Kansas City roots. At Hallmark, where job fit and company fit are critical components of a behavior-based selection process, consistently low turnover and high employee satisfaction prove the effectiveness of the company's hiring practices.

Tim Moran, corporate staffing director, recalls launching Behavior-Based Interviewing companywide more than 10 years ago. While the company's hiring record was good, it wanted to make it even better. The human resources group was constantly reading and learning about new methodologies, and what these people learned about Behavior-Based Interviewing seemed a great fit for their company. "Before, we were doing a lot of situational interviewing, asking fact-gathering and 'what-if' questions. But we liked the idea of benchmarking the process, and Behavior-Based Interviewing instantly made sense from a practical standpoint, basing future performance on past behavior."

The process began in the staffing group, where they investigated existing programs but decided to develop and implement the system on their own. They started by developing a competency dictionary and crafting questions to uncover facts about those competencies. Line managers throughout the company were also involved in this process. Over the course of about 6 months, they developed questions to assess both job competencies and fit with the unique company culture. Then they launched the program companywide—but that was just the beginning.

* Used with permission of Hallmark Cards, Incorporated.

Since then, there has been training and reinforcement to instill Behavior-Based Interviewing into the company's selection process. The results are great hires, low turnover, and a consistent approach to selecting employees, whether they are new college graduates or senior executives.

Hallmark has not implemented formal tracking of results from Behavior-Based Interviewing, so the evidence of its value has been anecdotal. According to Tim, "Line managers have been pleased with the structure and consistency of the approach." In several instances, following the disciplined process of Behavior-Based Interviewing has helped managers go beyond their initial impressions of a slate of candidates. By withholding judgment and seeking behavioral examples, in some cases they have found that their assumptions were false, and they have hired a different person from the one they originally favored.

Tim reports that one of the most helpful benefits of Behavior-Based Interviewing is that managers can find out how candidates deal with adverse circumstances. "All candidates will tell us about their positive aspects, but by asking them Behavior-Based questions, we can find out how they have handled conflict situations in the past, such as a challenging situation with a supervisor or a less-than-positive performance evaluation."

Day to day, this is how the selection process works at Hallmark. When a job becomes open, the position is posted internally. If there are no internal candidates, the staffing group holds a meeting with the line manager to review the job description, competencies, and results and behaviors he or she is looking for, then crafts the competencies, technical knowledge, and questions for Behavior-Based Interviewing. Résumés are solicited from a variety of channels, and candidate screening begins. Behavior-Based questions are used at every step of the process, right from the initial telephone screen; candidates who are selected for in-person interviews then undergo two to seven Behavior-Based Interviews before a decision is made. An interesting part of candidate selection at Hallmark is that everyone who comes in contact with a candidate—receptionists, administrative assistants, those observing a walk-through tour, and, of course, those interviewing the candidate—is encouraged to collect and share information about that candidate. "On more than one occasion," says Tim, "a person has treated our administrative staff poorly and has not been hired, no matter how great they were at every other stage of the interview. Their observable behaviors are used as evidence, just like the behaviors they report during their interviews."

Tim advises that the key to successful implementation of Behavior-Based Interviewing is commitment: commitment to training and commitment to making sure everyone in the organization understands why this process is being used. Further, the recruiting staff must "walk the talk" and be good examples for line managers.

In addition to providing training for line managers, Hallmark also requires its campus recruiters to participate in Behavior-Based Interview training. Often these campus recruiters are new hires who are just a few years out of college themselves and not yet at a managerial level. The training ensures that they are using consistent standards for judging candidates and are supporting their recommendations with behavioral examples. And because questions are based on job competencies and company fit, the Behavior-Based Interviewing approach ensures that these interviewers don't ask illegal or impolite or unprofessional questions. "We feel good about sending these folks out to represent us, knowing they are well prepared and will boost our company image," says Tim.

"In many ways, Behavior-Based Interviewing is harder work than going on 'gut feel,'" Tim comments. "Everyone must justify their Behavior-Based Interviewing evaluation. Particularly when interviewing candidates who are not good communicators or not that polished, we have to fight our instincts and withhold judgment. It's very easy to confuse good communication skills with good performance. But Behavior-Based Interviewing doesn't let us get away with that."

GE

Behavior-Based Interviewing is an integral part of every GE business worldwide. Established as a global training program about 10 years ago, Behavior-Based Interviewing supports the company imperative of "hiring the best" and puts a consistent face on decentralized recruiting and hiring programs that take place in diverse cultures around the world.

At GE, the bulk of the recruiting is done on college campuses by GE employees from the various lines of business. All recruiters are required to complete the Behavior-Based Interviewing training program before they can represent GE in this role. According to Judy Mebane, project leader for recruiting services, "Our training program ensures that everyone is delivering a consistent message, everyone under-stands and practices and knows how to execute Behavior-Based Inter-viewing when they go on campus." To date, GE has trained over 4000 people in Behavior-Based Interviewing.

Peter Bowen, manager of campus relations, recalls the beginnings of the program at GE. "We were beginning to recruit more heavily at undergraduate levels, to support our strategy of hiring more interns and co-op students as well as new graduates. We realized we had no corpo-ratewide benchmarks to ensure consistent quality in selecting these important employees, so we began to look at methods we could use. Behavior-Based Interviewing was the method we adopted."

GE developed and rolled out a day-and-a-half training program that includes foundational information and extensive practice to be sure the concepts are fully absorbed. All campus interviewers must com-plete the training program, but it's not enough just to go to the class. The instructor must certify that the individual has grasped the tech-niques and is prepared to use them effectively.

"Don't compromise the training course" is the advice given by Peter and Judy. Busy managers in the various businesses have sometimes requested that the time investment be scaled back, but corporate human resources has proved, time and time again, that less time is not suffi-cient to allow interviewers to truly internalize the concepts.

One of the most interesting aspects of Behavior-Based Interviewing at GE is its applicability across many different cultures. Some modifica-tions in the key competencies and interview questions are made to reflect cultural differences. But with only subtle variations, Behavior-Based Interviewing is relevant, effective, and applicable for all of GE's businesses in 100 countries around the world.

With a large recruiting force interacting with thousands of applicants every year, it is vital for GE that everyone adhere to legal interviewing guidelines. With its focus on performance in core competencies, Behavior-Based Interviewing is an ideal methodology for meeting this standard. GE is proud of its strong record of compliance, and in fact all of its global recruiting and hiring practices adhere to the stringent standards of U.S. laws.

The human resources organization at GE is a strong advocate for Behavior-Based Interviewing because it supports the goals of great-quality new hires, low turnover, and satisfied employees.

GE Aircraft Engines (GEAE)

GE's corporate human resources organization establishes the business practices and designs the training program. On the micro level, the practices and program are applied daily by individual businesses like GE Aircraft Engines—if you can call a multibillion-dollar global business with 26,000 employees "micro."

The sturdiness of Behavior-Based Interviewing and the GE training program are evident. Campus interviewers from all areas of GEAE complete the day-and-a-half program and visit some of the nation's top universities to recruit more than 400 interns, co-op students, and full-time employees each year. In the classroom, training is ingrained via extensive practice using both videotape and volunteer candidates.

According to Cheryl Brantmeier, manager of recruiting, staffing, and employment practice at GEAE, Behavior-Based Interviewing is extremely valuable for interviewers meeting with students, who typically have limited experience. "Our interviewers can ask them how they've dealt with situations and what they've done, whether on the job or in the classroom. The students should have some experience and examples that relate to their résumés. By asking for behavioral examples, we create a positive environment for the interview."

In addition to its universal application in the campus recruiting program, Behavior-Based Interviewing is also used when interviewing candidates for internal promotions and when bringing in experienced candidates from outside the company. Effects from the training filter up and throughout the company as campus interviewers move into hiring manager roles.

Building from the core training, GEAE has enhanced its Behavior-Based Interviewing program by providing online resources and e-learning components. According to Cheryl, these enhancements do not replace the classroom training; rather, they refresh and reinforce the learning and provide tools for hiring managers throughout the organization. For example, on the GEAE intranet there is a "staffing wizard" that a manager can use to review the interviewing process and gather sample questions. The extreme accessibility and usefulness of these tools fosters the strategic goals of digitizing business information and integrating best practices across the business.

Adopted as a universal business practice, Behavior-Based Interviewing has the versatility, flexibility, and integrity that are needed by a company as large and diverse as GE.

These six company stories demonstrate the proven value of Behavior-Based Interviewing in companies of all sizes in diverse industries. It provides a consistent, structured, *effective* method for selecting employees who are the right fit for the job and the company.

Notice how all of the companies emphasize training and consistent application as key to making the program thrive. As the leader and champion of Behavior-Based Interviewing at your company, be certain that you lay a foundation for success through a solid training program, and keep this program going strong even when the system has become well established. We'd love to profile *your* company as a shining success story in our next edition!

CHAPTER

6

A Review of Legal Guidelines for Interviewing Candidates

The law is the last result of human wisdom acting upon human experience for the benefit of the public.

—Samuel Johnson

T H E SOMETIMES CONFUSING and complex guidelines for conducting legal interviews are all designed with one purpose in mind: to eliminate bias, discrimination, prejudice, and unfair hiring practices and ensure that all candidates are judged solely on the basis of their ability to do the job. These guidelines stem from several pieces of legislation that have had a tremendous impact on hiring practices in the last half-century. Hard on the heels of this new consciousness of "fair hiring" has come increased conviction about the value of diversity in the workforce. Combined, these factors point to the undisputed need to establish equitable companywide hiring practices that build a strong and diverse workforce.

Good news! Behavior-Based Interviewing is inherently fair because it focuses on evaluating candidates' proven capabilities to meet predetermined job requirements. And having a planned, structured, even-handed approach to every step of the hiring process, from written job descriptions through interview questions and candidate evaluation, drastically reduces the opportunity for unintentional bias by interviewers who are using a more haphazard approach.

In conjunction with implementing Behavior-Based Interviewing, it is important to understand the legal guidelines for interviews and to know what constitute legal and illegal questions. The risks associated with illegal hiring—no matter how unintentional—are simply too high to ignore.

A Brief History

Beginning in the early 1960s, the United States government enacted several pieces of legislation prohibiting employment discrimination based on race, color, religion, sex, national origin, age, or disability. While this book is not intended to provide legal advice or to serve as an authoritative resource on government legislation, we do want to provide an overview of the relevant acts and how they relate to your hiring processes.

In brief:

- The Equal Pay Act of 1963 protects against sex-based wage discrimination.
- Title VII of the Civil Rights Act of 1964 prohibits employment discrimination based on race, color, religion, sex, or national origin.
- The Age Discrimination in Employment Act of 1967 protects individuals who are 40 years of age or older.
- Bias in hiring on the basis of pregnancy or childbirth is prohibited by the Pregnancy Discrimination Act of 1978.
- The Immigration Reform and Control Act of 1986 makes it illegal to employ aliens unless they have obtained permission to work in the United States.
- Title I and Title V of the Americans with Disabilities Act of 1990 prohibit employment discrimination against qualified individuals with disabilities.
- States, counties, and municipalities have also enacted their own rules for equitable hiring.

Penalties for discriminatory employment practices can be very steep. In the first three years of the twenty-first century, the U.S. Equal Employment Opportunity Commission (EEOC) filed more than 1100 suits alleging employment discrimination. These suits resulted in more than $1.5 billion in monetary benefits being awarded to plaintiffs. Of course, the legal fees and the time spent defending such a suit are added costs for the companies involved.

It is essential for managers at every company to understand all applicable fair employment rules and adhere to them at every step of the hiring process. For the latest and most complete information, contact the EEOC (www.eeoc.gov, telephone 202-663-4900) and your city, county, and state offices.

Implement Best Practices to Avoid Unintentional Discrimination

Many cases of potential discrimination occur as the result of careless, off-the-cuff questions asked by interviewers who are not aware of the guidelines. These kinds of questions can reveal information that may have an unconscious impact on the hiring decision. For example, knowing that one candidate is a homeowner while another rents an apartment might lead an interviewer to favor the homeowner because of the perceived value of "stability in the community." Other questions might feed into an interviewer's personal bias—against working mothers, for example, or people of a certain religion or culture.

The best way to avoid potential discrimination and its harmful consequences is to implement fair practices at every stage of the hiring process and to train and educate everyone involved in candidate interviewing and selection. Fortunately, Behavior-Based Interviewing promotes fair employment, and its structured process eliminates thoughtless and potentially risky activities.

The Benefits of Behavior-Based Questions

Begin by defining the essential functions of the job, developing a sound job description, and selecting interview questions. In Chapter 3, you learned how to develop job descriptions that reflect the essential functions of the position and the key competencies required. Interview questions based on these predetermined functions and competencies have several advantages:

1. They are entirely legal.
2. They yield valuable information that can be used to judge job candidates fairly.
3. They ensure equitable and consistent treatment of all candidates.

Behavior-Based questions focus the interview on the candidate's *ability* to perform essential functions rather than on his or her presumed *inability* to perform them as a result of his or her age, sex, disability, national origin, or any other factor.

When defining job functions, be certain that they truly are essential functions, not simply "the way it's always been done." For example, an inside salesperson might travel in her car to visit customers every few weeks. Before defining a driver's license, a vehicle, and the physical ability to travel to customer sites as part of the essential functions of the job, determine whether these visits are truly essential. Can contact be made by telephone? If that's the case, a person with physical disabilities that prevent him from traveling can be considered for the job. Can the visit frequency be reduced to once per quarter? A person who can travel only that often can now be considered for the job. Can the company supply the vehicle and possibly a driver? If so, a candidate who does not own a vehicle or possess a license will not be disqualified.

Equally important, be sure that interviewers don't make assumptions about candidates' abilities or disabilities. For example, you must not assume that a person who walks with a cane will not be able to handle a physical warehouse job, or that a young woman will have family/children issues that will prevent her from taking a job requiring travel. It's important that you phrase interview questions appropriately—and legally—with a focus on the ability to perform the defined job duties. Later in this chapter you'll find a table of legal and illegal interview questions related to all areas of possible discrimination. You can incorporate these into your training to be sure that all company interviewers, both human resources staff and hiring managers, understand how to phrase their questions to avoid assumptions, eliminate bias, and give all candidates an equal shot at the job.

Reasonable Accommodation

When you are considering essential functions and candidate abilities, you should be aware that the law requires companies to make "reasonable accommodation" to allow an otherwise qualified person to perform the essential functions of a job. As you will see in the list of legal and illegal questions later in this chapter, the need for accommodation should not be assumed, nor should interviewers inquire about the nature of any accommodation that might be needed. Medical examinations and disability-related inquiries are allowed *after* a conditional offer of employment is made.

If you are interviewing a candidate with an obvious disability, don't jump to conclusions about what the individual can and cannot do.

Instead, ask the candidate to demonstrate and/or describe how he would perform a specific job function. (Be sure you ask this question of *all* job candidates.) If the applicant indicates that he can perform a function "with reasonable accommodation," don't press to find out more; that issue is appropriately addressed only after an offer of employment has been made. At that point, the employer does have the right to determine the level of disability, the risk of performing certain tasks, and the accommodation that is necessary.

Some candidates might also require a reasonable level of accommodation during the selection process. The best way to address these needs without potentially discriminatory questioning is to inform *all* applicants, on the application form or during the preinterview screening, precisely what will be demanded of them during the selection process, then invite applicants to inform you if they will need accommodation to conform with these procedures. Here's an example of language you might use:

"All applicants will be required to take a physical tour of the warehouse. This involves walking approximately one-half mile on a level surface and ascending/descending a flight of 12 stairs. If, because of a disability, you require an accommodation to complete this tour, please advise the Human Resources representative at least 48 hours prior to your scheduled interview."

Train All Interviewers

Your predetermined list of Behavior-Based Interview questions, based on key competencies and essential job functions, is the core of an effective, legal interview. But don't neglect to train interviewers on the often less-structured opening, closing, and follow-up questions. Remember, off-the-cuff questioning is the most likely occasion for careless queries that are not within legal guidelines. Even the initial rapport-building questions should be preplanned to avoid straying into potentially risky discussions. Your interviewers do not have to follow a script for this initial dialogue. But they should be prepared with a list of "small-talk" openings that are friendly, help put the candidate at ease, yet do not invite unwanted information.

Here are a few examples of rapport-building questions and comments that, while seemingly harmless, might invite unwanted information that could lead to bias.

- "Oh, I see you went to Westgate High . . . I did too! What year did you graduate?"

- "Do you have any children?"
- "Where did you grow up?"
- "What an unusual name! What is its origin?"
- "I see you speak Farsi. How did you learn that?"
- "Tell me about some of the clubs you belong to and how you like to spend your free time."

Rather than risking bias or creating a stilted opening dialogue, encourage your interviewers to prepare their own list of approved questions that they will be comfortable using to break the ice with a candidate. A list of suggested questions is included in Chapter 4.

Of course, candidates may volunteer information that interviewers would prefer not to know. A candidate might apologize for being a few minutes late by explaining that her son's school bus was late *(potential for sex discrimination)*. Another job seeker might offer a behavioral example that occurred during his volunteer stint as a youth leader at his church, temple, or mosque *(potential for discrimination based on religion)*. When asked about education, a candidate might volunteer that he just attended his twenty-fifth college reunion *(potential for age discrimination)*. Interviewers should be trained to avoid comments and further questions about these topics if they are brought up by the candidate.

Treat All Candidates Consistently

You will ensure fairness if you create and follow a structured process for interviewing and selecting people for jobs. To be fair, the process needs to be the same for *all candidates*. In other words, you cannot make a requirement for one candidate that is not made for all others who are under consideration for the job.

Let's say you like to give an "in-box" test to managerial candidates to evaluate their ability to set priorities and manage multiple tasks. Legal hiring practices forbid you from deciding, willy-nilly, to administer this test to selected candidates. You can administer the test to *all* candidates, or (perhaps more sensibly) you can save this procedure for phase two of the interview process and then ask all remaining candidates to complete it.

Here's another example. Imagine you have a candidate whose accent tells you that she speaks English as a second language. You cannot devise a test of language skills for that candidate alone—for example, asking her how she would respond to a specific customer situation that might involve complex language. But you can ask that question of *all* candidates, provided that English language skills are an essential function of the job.

Use a Consistent Process to Evaluate Candidates

The best way to evaluate all candidates fairly is simply to follow the rating and evaluation process described in Chapter 3. The forms in Appendix 2 will guide you in assigning ratings to each candidate. These equitable ratings are not based on feelings, instincts, first impressions, or a great résumé, but rather on documented behaviors—SAR (situation, action, results) stories—that describe how an individual has actually accomplished something related to the defined job competencies. And because your process includes having all interviewers compare and discuss ratings, you employ another powerful tool to ensure that evaluations are fair and are based on documented performance.

Your role as a human resources professional or leader of hiring practices is to be sure that everyone sticks to the process. Be alert to the halo effect and the power of first impressions, and if you sense that others on the hiring team are being swayed by intangibles rather than by performance, bring the focus back to the documented examples uncovered during interviews. Keep pushing until team members can support their judgments with facts. Often just being "called" on this is enough to make the interviewer rethink a rating. Even if nothing is changed, the process reinforces the strength of your selection process. Remember, if your hiring decisions are not supported by documented performance, the validity and legality of your hiring process can be called into question.

Understand Legal and Illegal Questions

The EEOC guidelines cover a wide range of potentially discriminatory factors—race, color, religion, sex, national origin, age, and disability. Table 6-1 provides examples of legal and illegal questions for each area of potential discrimination. Exhibit 6-1 is a quiz that you can use to test your knowledge; feel free to incorporate this quiz into your interview training program.

If you are in doubt as to whether a question is legal, ask yourself whether the question relates to essential functions of the job. If it doesn't, don't ask the question.

Table 6-1
Legal and Illegal Questions

Inquiry Area	Illegal Questions	Legal Questions
Affiliations	• What clubs or social organizations do you belong to? • Do you belong to a union?	• What professional or trade groups do you belong to that you consider relevant to your ability to do this job?
Age	• How old are you? • What is your birth date? • When did you graduate?	• If you are hired, can you provide proof that you are at least 18 years of age? • If you are a minor, can you provide proof of age in the form of a work permit or other documentation? *(Age-related questions are allowable with minor candidates to be certain that they meet minimum age requirements for employment.)*
Alcohol or Drug Use	• How much do you drink? • Are you in a rehab program? • Have you ever had a drug or alcohol problem? • Have you ever been treated for drug or alcohol addiction?	• Do you currently use illegal drugs? *(Asking about the use of illegal drugs is not protected under the Americans with Disabilities Act.)*
Criminal Record	• Have you ever been arrested? • Have you ever been charged with a crime? *(Note the difference between "charged with" and "convicted of" a crime.)*	• Have you ever been convicted of a crime? *(If yes, you may ask for details, but the conviction can be used to deny a job only if it is directly related to performance of that job.)*

Culture / National Origin	• Are you a U.S. citizen?	• Upon employment, can you provide proof that you have the legal right to work in the United States?
	• Where were you born?	• What languages do you read/write/speak fluently? (*This question can be asked only if relevant to job performance.*)
	• What is your native language?	
	• What is the nationality of your parents/spouse?	
	• Are you a naturalized citizen? When did you become a citizen?	
	• Where did you grow up?	
	• What language do you speak at home?	
	• How did you learn [foreign language]?	
Disability	• Do you have any disabilities?	• Can you perform the functions of this job?
	• How is your health? How is your family's health?	• Can you demonstrate how you would perform the following job-related function?
	• When did you suffer your disability? How?	• As part of the hiring process, after a job offer has been made, you will be required to undergo a medical exam. (*To be legal, this must be required of all individuals who are offered employment at the company.*)
	• Have you had any recent illnesses or injuries?	
	• Will you please complete this medical history? (*You may ask for medical information only after a job offer has been made.*)	• Will you be able to perform these job functions with reasonable accommodation? (*May be asked only when the applicant has an obvious disability or has voluntarily disclosed a disability.*)
	• Do you need an accommodation to perform this job? (*This question can be asked only after a conditional job offer has been made.*)	• What was your attendance record at your last place of employment?
	• Have you ever filed a workers' compensation claim?	
	• How many days of work did you miss last year due to illness?	

(Continued)

Table 6-1
Legal and Illegal Questions (*Continued*)

INQUIRY AREA	ILLEGAL QUESTIONS	LEGAL QUESTIONS
Education	• Did you earn a GED? (*You should not ask about the nature of the high school diploma, but simply whether the candidate is a high school graduate if this is a requirement for the job.*) • When did you graduate?	• Questions related to degrees, courses, equivalent experience, or training that are related to job requirements.
Marital/Family Status	• Are you married? • What is your spouse's name? • What was your maiden name? • With whom do you live? • Do you have any children? How old are they? What are your child-care arrangements? • Do you plan to start a family soon? • Does your ex provide child support? • Where does your spouse work? • What benefits do you have through your spouse?	• Do you have relatives who work for this organization? If so, what are their names? • Do you anticipate any absences from work on a regular basis? If so, please explain the circumstances.

	Inadvisable	Advisable
Military	• Were you honorably discharged from the military? • Did you serve in the military of another country?	• In what branch of the armed services did you serve? • What type of training or education did you receive in the military?
Personal	• How much do you weigh? How tall are you? *(Questions about height and weight are permissible only if defined standards are essential for safe performance of the job.)* • Do you own or rent your home? • How is your credit rating? Do you have much outstanding debt? • Please provide a photograph for us to keep with your application.	• Are you able to [describe activity], which is an essential part of this job? • What is your present address? • This fiduciary position requires a clean credit rating. Will that be a problem for you?
Race/Color	• What is your race? • What color is your hair?/What color are your eyes?/What color is your skin?	• None
Religion	• What is your religious affiliation? • What church do you belong to? • What religious holidays do you observe? • Can you get a recommendation from your pastor, minister, or rabbi? • Does your religion permit you to work weekends?	• Are you available to work Saturday and Sunday shifts once per month? *(If applicable to the position.)*

(Continued)

Table 6-1
Legal and Illegal Questions (*Continued*)

INQUIRY AREA	ILLEGAL QUESTIONS	LEGAL QUESTIONS
Sex	• Are you male or female? (*This question should be avoided during the application and interview process unless it is an essential job requirement.*) • What are the names and relationships of the people who live with you? • Would you have a problem working with a female partner? • Are you comfortable in a gay-friendly environment? (*Any inquiries that are made of one sex but not the other are prohibited.*)	• Have you ever worked under a different name? (*Questions relating to an assumed name, changed name, or nickname that are necessary to enable a check on work record and education record are permissible.*)

Exhibit 6-1 Exercise—A Quiz on Legal Interview Questions

Test your knowledge of legal and illegal interview questions. Check the appropriate box to indicate whether you believe the question can legally be asked during an interview. An answer guide with explanation is provided after the quiz.

LEGAL	ILLEGAL	QUESTION
☐	☒	1. Because this project is estimated to last at least 18 months, we need to know if you are planning to take any maternity leave in the next 2 years.
☒	☐	2. This job requires fluency in Spanish. Are you fluent?
☐	☐	3. Are you legally entitled to work in the United States?
☐	☒	4. From your résumé, I noticed that you are actively involved in your church. Would it be a problem for you to work on Sundays?
☒	☐	5. This job requires you to move 30-pound packages from one area to another. Are you able to do that with or without reasonable accommodation?
☐	☒	6. How many sick days did you take last year?
☒	☐	7. In your job you will handle large sums of money. Have you ever been arrested for stealing?
☒	☐	8. This job requires you to travel overnight about 2 days per week and to attend out-of-town conferences once per month. Does this travel schedule present a problem for you?
☐	☒	9. This job requires that you relocate. Is your wife okay with that?
☐	☒	10. What kind of reasonable accommodation would you need in order to perform this job function?
☐	☒	11. What are your child-care arrangements?
☐	☒	12. What kind of work does your husband do?
☐	☒	13. Are you in good health?
☐	☒	14. What is your marital status?
☐	☒	15. Have you ever filed a workers' compensation claim?

(Continued)

Exhibit 6-1 (*Continued*)

LEGAL	ILLEGAL	QUESTION
☐	☐	16. This position requires you to be in front of customers all day. Would you be able to lose 5 or 10 pounds before starting?
☐	☐	17. I see you use a wheelchair. This job will require you to be out of the office meeting with clients several days per week. Can you tell me how you would get around?
☐	☐	18. Tell me about your disability. How long have you been disabled?
☐	☐	19. This is a nonsmoking workplace. Will that be a problem for you?
☐	☐	20. How many days of work have you missed over the past year?
☐	☐	21. We like our salespeople to play golf with customers. Do you belong to any country clubs?
☐	☐	22. Do you have a disability that would prevent you from performing the essential functions of this job?
☐	☐	23. Most of the people who work here are Hispanic. Do you think you'd have any trouble fitting in?
☐	☐	24. When did you last have a physical exam?
☐	☐	25. We don't require a photograph, but if you want to supply one to help us keep track of who's who, that would be fine.
☐	☐	26. Do you smoke?

Answer Guide

LEGAL	ILLEGAL	EXPLANATION
☐	☑	1. No questions related to pregnancy are permitted.
☑	☐	2. This question is allowable because it pertains to essential job functions.

Exhibit 6-1 (Continued)

Legal	Illegal	Explanation
☑	☐	3. It is the employer's responsibilty to ensure that only legal workers are hired, but a better wording of this question would be, "If we were to employ you, could you provide proof that you are eligible to work in the United States?"
☐	☑	4. However, if weekend work is an essential component of the job, rephrase the question ("This position requires work on Sundays. Is that a problem for you?"), and it is perfectly legal.
☑	☐	5. In the interview stage, do *not* probe to find out what "reasonable accommodation" might be needed; defer this line of questioning until after you have made a conditional offer of employment.
☐	☑	6. Worded this way, the question invites probing into the areas of health and disability.
☐	☑	7. You may inquire only about *convictions*, not arrests.
☑	☐	8. This is a bona fide requirement for this job; thus the question is legal.
☐	☑	9. Don't have open discussions about a candidate's family situation. You may, of course, ask if the *candidate* would be OK with relocation.
☐	☑	10. Don't inquire about the details of the accommodation; you should simply ask if the individual can do the job "with or without" reasonable accommodation.
☐	☑	11. This question is not relevant to job performance.
☐	☑	12. This question is not relevant to job performance.
☐	☑	13. This question might open an inquiry into disability.
☐	☑	14. This question is not relevant to job performance.
☐	☑	15. This question might invite bias-related information.
☐	☑	16. This so-called requirement is not relevant to job performance.

(Continued)

Exhibit 6-1   (Continued)

Legal	Illegal	Explanation
☑	☐	17. It is allowable to ask a candidate how she would perform an essential job function. It is also okay to refer to her disability because it is clearly visible.
☐	☑	18. Keep any disability-related questions in the realm of job performance.
☑	☐	19. Note that you do not inquire whether the individual smokes, but simply whether he can conform to the required workplace environment.
☑	☐	20. It is legal to check attendance record as long as you do not attempt to tie attendance to health or disability.
☐	☑	21. Golf is not a bona fide job requirement, and probing into personal affiliations is not allowed.
☐	☑	22. Instead, after explaining the essential functions of the job, ask if the individual can perform them "with or without reasonable accommodation."
☐	☑	23. This is not an appropriate way to establish "organization fit" and might invite discrimination.
☐	☑	24. This question might be seen as an attempt to gather information about health or disability.
☐	☑	25. Photographs of candidates may not be collected because they can affect any number of areas of potential bias.
☐	☑	26. This question is not relevant to job performance.

Remember that the purpose of hiring guidelines and legislation is to eliminate bias and ensure fair hiring practices for all candidates. When you use Behavior-Based Interviewing techniques, you automatically promote fair hiring. Just be certain that your practices cover all areas of the interview process and that you train all interviewers to recognize and avoid illegal questions. The end result will be hiring decisions that are based on the ability to perform essential functions of the job—exactly the intent of the legislation. As you can see, Behavior-Based Interviewing is a solid cornerstone of equitable hiring.

Conduct Effective Interviews Regardless of How Candidates Prepare

*If each of us hires people who are smaller than we are, we shall become
a company of dwarfs. But if each of us hires people who are bigger than
we are, we shall become a company of giants.*

—David Ogilvy

HAVE YOU EVER INTERVIEWED a candidate who had a
perfect response for every question you asked? Not only that, she introduced herself effectively and closed your meeting professionally, and
even if you weren't using Behavior-Based Interview questions, she gave
you specific examples of ways in which she had used her skills in the past.

On the flip side, you've probably interviewed dozens of candidates
who don't know much about your company and ramble on about unre-
lated subjects. When you ask for a specific example, they give you a
blank stare or talk about what they "would" do or "always" do; even
when prompted, they have a hard time recounting an SAR story. The
difference between these two candidates is interview preparation.

Such preparation can take many forms, such as reading books and
articles on interview skills, practicing with a friend or relative, working

with a professional interview coach, or videotaping practice interviews to critique the message and delivery. There are many, many good resources that are easily available to candidates today.

What does this mean to you as a company interviewer? Should you be wary of candidates who seem *too* well prepared? Should you worry that candidates have rehearsed answers that present only the positive facets of their background or that tell you what they think you want to hear? What can you do to be sure you are getting real, honest answers and uncovering the candidate's true potential? And finally, how can you get this same information from *un*prepared candidates?

In this chapter we'll discuss a variety of ways in which candidates prepare for their interviews, tell you the possible dangers and oversights you should look for, and give you some ideas for uncovering the full story.

As discussed in Chapter 3, when you begin interviewing, you should share with the candidates what will take place. Explain that you will be asking for specific examples of things they have done, and explain the SAR format. You should also tell candidates that you may follow up their answers with some additional (probing) questions because you want to be sure you are getting all the relevant facts. Finally, try to put candidates at ease. Tell them that you'll give them some time to recall specific examples and not to worry if something doesn't come to mind immediately. By preparing candidates with this information up front, you will minimize their stress and improve their ability to provide information to you in the way that you request.

Behavior-Based Interviewing Helps You Avoid Rehearsed Answers

In many ways, Behavior-Based Interviewing solves a lot of interviewing dilemmas. Because you are asking for specific examples from the candidate's history, it is difficult for him to "fake it" by giving rehearsed answers or telling you what he thinks you want to hear. And by asking follow-up probing questions, you will be sure to get the full SAR story and possibly uncover some of the less-positive details that the candidate has withheld from the initial answer.

For the candidate, too, Behavior-Based Interviewing makes the process less stressful and more enjoyable. Instead of struggling to figure out what you want to hear, the candidate can simply tell you what she has done in specific competency areas that are relevant to the job. Most candidates will use the SAR story format more and more naturally as the interview progresses, and as their confidence builds, they'll relax and be able to relate more naturally to the interviewer.

Three Interview Stories

In the following stories, you'll read about three candidates who prepared for their interviews in three different ways. Key points are followed by an "Interviewer's Tip"—suggestions for interpreting the candidate's response, structuring interview programs, and digging beneath the candidate's answers to be sure that you are getting the complete story, not one that has been masked by interview preparation.

Aaron—Preparing on His Own

Aaron was contacted by the inside recruiter for a large manufacturing firm within his industry. He was not actively looking for a job, but after some thought he decided to consider the opportunity to see if it offered long-term career advantages.

Research

Before his first in-person interview, Aaron found out as much as he could about the company. He scoured the company's website, reviewed its annual report, and searched for recent news articles. Because this company was a direct competitor of his current employer, he knew a bit about some of the market and manufacturing challenges it was facing, and he prepared questions about how the company intended to address these challenges.

Interviewer's Tip

Good candidates are as concerned as you are about company fit and job fit. If you encounter a candidate who has clearly done his homework and asks you probing questions about the company's direction, values, culture, and strategic plans, answer these questions seriously and with as much candor as possible. Don't gloss over or minimize any problem areas. Top performers are interested in coming in and solving problems—these challenges excite them. Their areas of concern are usually related to the company's real commitment to solving the problems and the resources they will have available to make change happen. So be sure to share this information as well.

Practice

Next, Aaron worked on his presentation and delivery. He was accustomed to giving executive-level presentations in his current position, so he felt quite comfortable talking about the technical nature of his job and with his overall presentation style. But because he hadn't interviewed for a job for a long time, he wanted to practice answering the "tough" questions, such as what his salary requirements were and why he was considering leaving his current employer after nearly 20 years. He also wanted to be sure that he wasn't too startled by any of the questions that might be asked, so he reviewed a book on executive interviewing to become familiar with the typical range of questions. Finally, he role-played with his wife to build his comfort level in delivering his planned responses.

Interviewer's Tip

Sometimes a candidate has a pretty basic reason for making a move. He might be looking for more money. He may have been passed over for promotion and may want to get to the next level. Perhaps he feels that "newer blood" gets more appreciation than he does. Or he may just be fishing to find out his value in the marketplace—and the package will have to be pretty compelling to get him to accept the job. Candidates who prepare will have positive, credible answers to the question, "Why are you leaving your current job?" They might tell you that they are looking for more challenge or a greater chance to make a difference—and this could very well be the most important factor in making a change. Others who are less prepared may blurt out an answer that reveals less altruistic reasons. Don't judge the unprepared candidate too harshly because of this kind of response. Use your Behavior-Based Interviewing questions to uncover his track record—how he's behaved in the past, how he's handled difficult people situations or work challenges, and how he's reacted when things haven't gone his way. Questions like these will help you delve beneath the immediate answer from both practiced and unpracticed candidates:

- "Tell me about a time when your manager didn't agree with an idea of yours. What did you do? What was the result?"
- "Most of us have experienced personality conflicts with a boss at some time in our careers. Describe a recent situation in which you

found that your style clashed with your boss's. How did that affect your performance?"
- "Describe a recent situation in which you became frustrated at work."
- "Tell me about a performance evaluation that pointed out a development need. How did your manager present this to you? How did that make you feel? What did you do about it, and what was the result?"
- "Describe a situation in which someone who you felt was not deserving was promoted. How did that make you feel? Did you speak with anyone about it?"

Unless a candidate is totally unprofessional in his response ("My boss is a jerk"), you can accept a less-than-perfect answer to the "Why are you leaving?" question that often takes the less-prepared candidate by surprise.

Assessment

Through meetings with Human Resources and several senior managers, Aaron gained a great deal of information about the company, his prospective role in it, and how he would fit into the organization, both immediately and in the long term. After the interview, he scrutinized this information carefully and talked over various scenarios with his wife. This would be a big move for them and a significant career transition for him. He was invited back for several additional interviews, and each time he gained more information and asked more searching questions. He wanted to be absolutely certain that the move was right for him before he jumped.

Interviewer's Tip

Particularly with a candidate who is currently employed, you might feel that you are as much "under the microscope" as the candidate is. After all, this candidate doesn't have the same compelling reason to take the job as someone who is unemployed. The best thing you can do is provide a realistic yet optimistic outlook. Don't be afraid to share your enthusiasm for the company and its future. Talk about the many things your company does well, how it treats employees, and the kind of culture it has. But stop short of overpersuading a candidate. Let him make the decision about where he will be happiest and most productive.

With this individual—the candidate who's pretty happy where he is—it's particularly important to use Behavior-Based Interviewing questions to assess job fit and company fit carefully, for it is these factors that are most critical for employee satisfaction and retention. Chapter 4 contains sample questions that relate solely to job fit and company fit. You can use them as is or tailor them for your own company and culture.

Outcome

Aaron received an attractive offer but elected not to take the new position. In the end, it came down to job fit. He felt the new position was too much like his current role and did not represent his ideal career path. He did, however, gain tremendous respect for the company and its people. Because he handled the process frankly and professionally, he did not "burn his bridges" and would be considered for another opportunity with the company—one that might be more in line with his long-term career goals.

Interviewer's Tip

If you are actively recruiting candidates from your competition, don't look only at people who do the particular job you're trying to fill. Look for people with related experience or those who are one step below the current role. You might find that candidates are more eager to make a move if the job represents a true challenge.

Sandra—Working with an Interview Coach

Sandra began an active job search when the management consulting firm where she had worked for the past two years experienced a sharp decline in business coinciding with an economic downturn. Her expertise was business development and growth/turnaround strategy.

Sandra gave a good deal of thought to her career move. Although she had enjoyed consulting, she decided that she wanted to return to a corporate environment, where she would be able to implement the strategies she developed and be there to celebrate the results. She wanted to be part of an organization that had a genuine commitment to improvement, change, and growth. Through research and networking, she learned about a leadership-development rotational program being launched at a major corporation that was "reinventing" itself under a new executive team. This seemed an ideal match for her personal goals, so she submitted her résumé via the company's website and was thrilled when she was called in for an interview.

Preparation

Sandra had worked with a professional résumé writer/career coach who had done a great job of pulling out her verifiable accomplishments and presenting them on her résumé. Now she decided to engage the coach's services for interview preparation. A central component of this coaching was developing what the coach called "CAR stories"—stories highlighting Sandra's career achievements using a Challenge–Action–Results format.

Interviewer's Tip

The SAR (situation-action-result) story format used in Behavior-Based Interviewing is a staple of professional career advice. It might be called by a different name, but its components are the same. Here are several commonly used acronyms and their meanings:

- CAR: Challenge—Action—Result
- SCAR: Situation or Challenge—Action—Result
- SPAR: Situation—Problem—Action—Result
- STAR: Situation or Task—Action—Result
- 3C: Circumstances/Challenges—Conduct—Conclusion

Well-prepared candidates will be very comfortable delivering answers in your requested SAR format and will have worked to prepare a number of these stories related to each of their past positions, the areas that they perceive to be their core competencies, and the key points identified in the job description or advertisement. Because interviews can be stressful, some candidates might feel panicky if you ask them for an SAR example documenting a competency that they haven't prepared for or if you ask probing questions as a follow-up to an answer they have prepared. If a candidate goes from confident to panic-stricken, don't assume that she has something to hide. Give her at least 10 seconds to collect her thoughts, and offer to go back to that question at a later time if she's still drawing a blank. Don't make her feel that she's failed the interview. Just move on to your next question and go back to that area at the end if you still need SAR examples to complete the Interview Guide for a key competency.

Grueling Interview

Sandra spent nearly 5 hours at the company, interviewed with several people, and performed a variety of tasks and tests, including a math and critical reading assessment, a role-play problem-solving situation, and an "in-box" test of her ability to prioritize. At one point she sat with two Human Resources representatives and answered a number of Behavior-Based Interviewing questions. Because of her work with her coach, this was one of the least taxing parts of her day. All in all, Sandra felt that the questions she was asked and the tasks demanded of her were quite challenging but thorough and fair, a reasonably close simulation of the situations she would face if she were selected for the position.

Interviewer's Tip

Asking candidates to actually perform a test or demonstration is an excellent way to assess their competency. A simulation that is close to real work demands will be most valuable. Of course, to meet legal hiring guidelines, it is essential that these tasks are required of all candidates. In Sandra's case, she had gone through several telephone interviews before her in-person meeting, and all candidates who were invited to the company were given the same set of challenges. At this company, Behavior-Based Interviewing was just one tool in the selection process. To make this tool as valuable as possible at your company, be sure to assign different Behavior-Based Interviewing questions to different interviewers, then meet to compare notes on candidates' responses and SAR stories.

Executive Interview

Sandra was invited to return for a final interview with the senior vice president. At this one-on-one meeting, she learned about the corporate strategy behind the new leadership initiative. When asked for her comments and input, she used CAR/SAR stories to show how she had responded to challenges such as financial turnaround, culture shift, and leadership of cross-functional team initiatives. At the end of the meeting, Sandra remained very excited about the opportunity. She believed that the new executive team was clearly committed to the change process.

Interviewer's Tip

Well-prepared candidates who understand the power of SAR statements will take every opportunity to drop one into an interview response. They know that a documented example of something that they have done is more compelling than a nonspecific "would/could/should" statement. Think of these candidates as prepared rather than rehearsed. They have delved into their memory banks to find specific examples of ways they have behaved in the past that support their core competencies. They may even have practiced their responses. But the fact is that they are not spouting memorized, "canned" responses to "typical" interview questions, especially when you follow up with probing questions. Instead, they are sharing stories that are factual and that support their candidacy.

Be sure that you ask them to give you examples with negative as well as positive consequences—for example, "Tell me about a time when you were unable to accomplish a goal. Why were you unsuccessful? What could you have done differently?" Another good idea is to give candidates the opportunity to add examples to any traditional or situational questions you might ask. For example, let's say you ask the situational interview question, "How would you describe your ideal boss?" to gather information about job fit. You can ask for follow-up information in either a negative or a positive format: "Which of your past bosses was most like your ideal? Which was least like?" You will probably gain some valuable information. You might have to prompt less-prepared candidates to give you examples or tell you stories. With both groups, be sure to probe to get the full story if a complete SAR statement is not delivered.

Outcome

Sandra was offered and accepted the position. About 9 months later, she contacted her résumé writer/coach to update her résumé—not because she was looking for a new job, but because she was being recruited internally to join the management team of one of the functional areas of the company. Again she peppered her résumé with achievement statements (abbreviated SARs) and prepared for her interviews by brushing up on her presentation and storytelling techniques.

Interviewer's Tip

Even when you are recruiting internal candidates and promoting current employees, use Behavior-Based Interviewing to uncover a candidate's full range of competencies or improvement needs. Don't simply assume that you "know" this person or that she possesses the full range of required skills. Ask for SARs that represent competencies that have not been witnessed on the job or documented in a performance appraisal. Your internal recruiting/promotion screening should be just as rigorous as your external recruiting, so that the people who advance have a strong likelihood of being successful.

Alex—Learning with a Group

As part of his severance package following a major downsizing, Alex received outplacement support. His package of services included one-on-one résumé assistance and group training sessions that covered many aspects of a job search, including interviewing. In addition, he could call on his counselor for individual help with specific problems that he encountered during his transition.

Group Interview Training

Alex took part in a daylong program devoted to building interview skills. First the group watched a video, then a facilitator led a discussion of interviewing etiquette, responses to typical questions, appropriate follow-up, and other areas of interview activity. Candidates were coached on preparing a 90-second introduction as a response to the frequent introductory question, "So, tell me about yourself," and were also advised to close an interview appropriately by asking about the next step. Key points that were covered included how to explain why you left your position, how to deal with an unstructured interviewer who seemed to have no agenda, and how to perform well in a telephone screening interview. A variety of interview types were discussed—sequential (meeting individually with one person after another), panel or team (a group interview, often with cross-functional team members), confrontational/stress (when the interviewer attempts to unbalance the candidate to see how he or she reacts), and Behavior-Based.

Interviewer's Tip

In Chapter 3 we recommend communicating to each candidate the agenda and structure of your interview. Candidates have heard so much information about interviewing that they might be wondering what will hit them next! Knowing what to expect does a lot to calm their nerves and lets them focus on the messages they are trying to deliver.

Group Training on SARs

In Alex's group training session, the facilitator did a good job of explaining how to describe examples using a storytelling technique that followed the SAR format. Repeatedly, the participants were urged to go back to the work they had done on their résumés. At this firm, one of the key components in résumé development is preparing numerous SARs, which then, of course, can be used in interviews as well as on the résumé.

Interviewer's Tip

As you evaluate candidates' responses, be sure that the examples provided are truly responsive to the competency area you are assessing at the time. For example, let's say you are attempting to evaluate writing skills, and you ask a candidate to "describe the most difficult writing assignment you ever had." In response, the candidate tells a good, solid SAR story that illuminates time-management or priority-setting skills. You will need to ask another Behavior-Based or probing question to assess this candidate's written communications skills.

Dealing with Difficult Questions

The group was coached on how to deal with typical and challenging questions, both traditional and Behavior-Based. Many of these questions are designed to uncover job-fit and company-fit data as well as job skills. Examples include, "What is your greatest weakness?" "Explain how you handled a stressful situation." "Tell me about a recent disagreement with your boss and how you handled it." The group discussed ways in which they might respond to these questions, including sharing weaknesses that are irrelevant to the job and showing how they had learned, grown, or improved as the result of an error.

Interviewer's Tip

Candidates try to anticipate any kind of interview question, and often they will practice responses to what they consider challenging questions. But you will find that Behavior-Based Interviewing will enable you to get true responses if you ask for multiple SARs that illuminate a candidate's true motivations. Remember also that the motivational-fit questions are an excellent tool for distinguishing the best candidate among a slate of several with strong qualifications. The right candidate will be highly motivated by the job environment and company culture.

Communications Style

One of the more controversial areas of Alex's group training was a presentation on personality and communications styles. Candidates were encouraged to build rapport by modeling their communications style on that of the interviewer. For example, if the interviewer is thorough and detail-oriented, be sure to provide detail in your SAR stories. On the other hand, if the interviewer seems more "big picture" or glosses over details, you can do the same and present just the highlights of your SARs. If your interviewer is warm and empathetic, you may want to speak more freely about your own feelings than you would if the interviewer appeared formal and businesslike. Alex's group debated this topic quite vigorously. Some felt that it was dishonest to adopt a communications style that was not their own, and that doing so would backfire when they took the job. Others argued that adapting their style simply meant doing a better job of communicating according to the individual preferences of your audience.

Interviewer's Tip

Behavior-Based Interviewing is a terrific tool for removing personality issues from the decision-making process. Whether interviewers bond with a candidate or not, they must back up their recommendations with specific examples that prove job competencies. This interview structure ensures that you base your evaluation of someone as a "great communicator" not on your rapport with that person, but rather on documented examples.

Outcome

Alex pursued his job search vigorously and quickly turned up several good job possibilities. Within a few months, he was hired by an insurance company as part of its application-development organization. The company did not use Behavioral-Based Interviewing, but relied instead on situational questions that asked Alex how he "would" perform on the job and with a group. On the job, Alex found that he had underestimated the importance of teamwork within the development group. While Alex could work with teams, when tackling difficult challenges he was most productive working alone. He adapted by taking problems home and working on them there, then coming in and presenting his solutions during team meetings. Nearing burnout, he approached his manager and "came clean." He was assigned small projects that he could work on independently; however, his growth potential was severely limited as a result. From the security of his existing position, he launched a new search and left the company about 18 months after joining it.

Interviewer's Tip

Behavior-Based Interviewing would have prevented this situation. The interviewer would have noticed a trend in Alex's stories that pointed away from working in a team environment and great success when working alone. Because team skills were a true essential, Alex would not have been selected for the position. As an interviewer, be sure to solicit enough Behavior-Based examples to put together a complete and accurate picture of the candidate. Watch for contradictory trends and statements, and keep asking for specific examples to allay any concerns or red flags. Finally, do a thorough reference check, probing specifically into your areas of concern. In fact, you can ask Behavior-Based questions to encourage the reference to provide specific examples that support a candidate's competencies.

Be Ready for Practiced and Unpracticed Candidates

It's a pleasure to interview candidates who have researched, prepared, and practiced. They are usually comfortable and confident, and they give you the information you need to make a good hiring decision. For the most part, they are as concerned as you are with finding the right fit. But beware of those candidates who are more concerned about landing any job than about finding the right job. Keep asking for Behavior-Based examples that demonstrate core competencies, not irrelevant skills, and be on the lookout for gaps in their background or trends that contradict their statements.

**Showstopper: The Candidate Can't Answer
Behavior-Based Questions**

As an interviewer, you probably dread those occasions when a job candidate just can't come up with good SAR stories. No matter what question you ask, the candidate freezes up and just can't remember. This can happen with highly prepared as well as with unprepared candidates. You know from the résumé or application that the candidate has relevant experience. You're pretty sure that the SAR stories exist, but the candidate can't recall them. What do you do? Try these tips.

- Wait it out a bit. Give candidates at least 10 seconds to think of an example before you move on to the next question.
- Assure candidates that they can go back to a question if they think of something later. Be positive and reassuring even if they've failed to provide an example.
- Get the candidate talking about anything related to the job. Follow the candidate's cues and insert a Behavior-Based question whenever you can. Encourage the candidate to continue, using these kinds of questions and comments:
  - "Tell me more about that."
  - "It sounds like you enjoyed that."
  - "Describe a typical day on the job. What kinds of problems and challenges did you face?"
  - "What was tough about the job? How did you handle it?"
  - "How did you learn to do that?"
  - "How were you selected for that job?"
- Follow up your open-ended question with specific probes once you are able to elicit a specific example rather than a general response.

Candidates who have not prepared present a different set of challenges. Be patient and give them ample opportunity to recall SAR stories that showcase their competencies. Don't downgrade them too severely for gauche answers, and build their confidence through clear communication and rapport.

Whether your candidates are well or ill prepared, you can rely on Behavior-Based Interviewing as the foundation for gaining valuable information and accurately assessing each one's competencies and potential.

Implementing a Behavior-Based Interviewing Program at Your Company

In a time of drastic change it is the learners who inherit the future. The learned usually find themselves equipped to live in a world that no longer exists.

—Eric Hoffer

NOW THAT YOU HAVE learned how and why your company will benefit from a Behavior-Based Interviewing program, you are ready to begin the implementation process. This chapter will tell you how to do it so that the program is successfully launched and consistently applied and thus becomes a valuable and integral part of your company's selection processes.

This chapter is intended for the senior managers and human resources staff who will be given the task of designing the program and leading the roll-out. In addition to giving you a blueprint for implementation, we have identified a variety of "showstoppers" that can derail, obstruct, or halt your program before or after its implementation. Be alert for these potential roadblocks and disruptions. If you find that some of them are present at your company, use our tips to overcome, avoid, or resolve the problems before they affect the success of your Behavior-Based Interviewing program and the results it will bring to your company.

Implement Your Program Top to Bottom

In Chapter 5 you read vignettes on companies that have successfully implemented Behavior-Based Interviewing. In each case, the company went to great lengths to ensure that communication, training, and support for the program were instilled in every area of the operation. You can learn from these examples. If a Behavior-Based Interviewing program is not properly rolled out to all managers in every department that is involved in hiring, mistakes will continue to be made, steps will be skipped, inconsistencies will develop, and bad hiring decisions will persist. Consider these four examples:

- In a medium-sized business, four out of five marketing divisions hiring entry-level salespeople adopted Behavior-Based Interviewing because of forecasts of high employee attrition. The fifth division chose to continue to use its preferred "most like me" method of hiring. The top executive of this division had played football in college and hired only star athletes from the Big Ten schools. After a few years, the four divisions using Behavior-Based Interviewing saw a 93 percent retention rate for their newly hired sales force. The division that elected not to use Behavior-Based Interviewing posted an 86 percent retention rate during this same period of time. This percentage difference might not sound like much, but when it was translated into the costs associated with making a hiring mistake, such as rehiring and retraining, the price tag was a startling seven-digit number. The ex-football player executive was sold by this news and immediately implemented Behavior-Based Interviewing. A year later, his top rookie sales representatives were neither athletes nor from a Big Ten school.
- A rapidly expanding technology company rolled out Behavior-Based Interviewing but did not make the training sessions mandatory. Only those managers who wanted to attend the training sessions participated, and no provision was made for making up

the sessions. A candidate who interviewed with this company tells this story: "The interviewer did all the talking during our 45-minute session and asked me only one question, which was, 'How does your work experience relate to the position that I've just described?' The interviewer seemed to be in a real bind and in a rush to hire someone because his department wasn't producing results." In some areas of this company, Behavior-Based Interviewing techniques are properly used, but companywide there is a lack of consistency in applying the techniques and using the program. Major issues are at stake—several key organizational areas are attracting talent from the best business schools, but they aren't properly collecting the facts they need to determine whether these candidates are the best job fit and company fit. This start-up company has limited resources and operates at a very fast pace, and hiring mistakes can easily cripple its operations. Finding the right-fit candidates who can thrive in this type of environment is critical to its success.

- A professional services company used a memo to announce the decision to adopt Behavior-Based Interviewing—no other discussion or ownership or training was provided for. The memo included a list of interview questions to ask and some guidelines about what to look for in a candidate. At this company, the process is for interviewers to get together after full days of interviews to discuss their findings for each candidate. The manager with the most authority listens to everyone's input, and then weights his opinion above everyone else's to make the final decision. Even though some steps in a Behavior-Based Interviewing program are followed, the top manager still makes the decision based on gut feeling. In addition, his habit of not fully considering the other interviewers' input has begun to have a demoralizing effect on them. They find themselves spending valuable time following a process and providing input that is often ignored or overridden. Not only that, but this is a billable-hour environment, and they are required to make up the time they spend interviewing. You can imagine that they are devoting less and less time and attention to the Behavior-Based Interviewing process, thus diminishing its effectiveness even further.

- At a Fortune 500 company, the CFO mandated that every manager throughout the organization learn and use Behavior-Based Interviewing. What was important to this executive was the quality of the hires and how employees were treated after they were brought on board. When the CFO left the organization, however, everyone began looking for shortcuts. Gradually, the number of Behavior-Based Interviews was reduced. Fewer managers participated in the interview process for each candidate. Review sessions were shortened, and some managers even skipped them, "mailing in" their recommendations but not being fully involved in the selection process. Over time, this lack of attention and commitment began to affect the effectiveness of this company's system and thus the fit and retention of its new hires. This is an example of why many champions at every level are needed to promote the effort on a consistent basis.

These four examples are alarming and clearly illustrate that hiring mistakes can still occur even when Behavior-Based Interviewing has been implemented. The rest of this chapter will provide you with ways to successfully implement Behavior-Based Interviewing throughout your organization so that everyone who is involved in hiring at any level will begin to use this process proficiently and consistently. A successful and deep-rooted implementation of this process is the only way to have a major impact to a company's bottom line and significantly reduce the cost of hiring mistakes, as discussed in Chapter 1. To meet the financial and strategic objectives of a Behavior-Based Interviewing program, there must be a total commitment to the program and the implementation plan so that your target audience—all personnel involved in hiring—will embrace the ideas and concepts and execute them.

The steps in a successful companywide implementation are

1. Identify barriers to change.
2. Start with a vision—use a business case to create uneasiness.
3. Obtain the support of leaders and champions.
4. Communicate and sell.
5. Create corporate standards and common materials.
6. Train and follow up.
7. Measure and evaluate.

Identify Barriers to Change

Every organization has its own unique culture, and also its own obstacles and barriers to change initiatives. You'll have an easier time implementing a change in your interviewing policy if you take the time to understand what those barriers are, anticipate any criticism of or opposition to this policy that people might have, and prepare to handle and overcome the obstacles you will encounter. A good way to start is to review the activities and strategies used in recent successful change initiatives and use those same strategies for the change to Behavior-Based Interviewing. Determine what steps made those efforts successful and how barriers to change were overcome in those situations. Past change initiatives can work in your favor by paving the way for new changes and by giving you an understanding of what works at your company.

Showstopper: Barriers to Change

- There is insufficient support from top management.
- Change is not mandated.
- Too many change initiatives are going on simultaneously—a "flavor of the month" syndrome.
- Not enough resources and time are invested to support the effort.
- There is too much comfort with the status quo.
- There is fear of the unknown.
- The vision is inconsistent.
- Communications are poor.
- Training is insufficient.
- There is a lack of understanding of the need for the change.
- There is inconsistent commitment from the people who do the hiring.
- Cultural issues undermine support and buy-in.

Each of these roadblocks can be avoided or overcome with a well-planned, thoroughly executed, well-supported program. This chapter takes you step by step through implementation, and you will avoid many of these obstacles simply by following the plan. Further, by understanding the unique barriers that are present within your company, you can take preemptive action to avoid many of the showstoppers right from the start.

Start with a Vision—Use a Business Case to Create Uneasiness

Get attention and create urgency by shocking people into understanding why a change in the way they interview needs to take place and by creating a dissatisfaction and uneasiness with the way things are. Chapter 1 details ways to create this uneasiness by analyzing just how much it costs to make one bad hiring decision. You can make a grand statement by multiplying the cost of one hiring mistake by the total number of hiring mistakes that have occurred in your company in the past and that you anticipate may be made in the following years. This is particularly meaningful to upper management in all areas of the company, as they can appreciate the financial implications of poor hiring. The exercise in Chapter 1 will also create a very telling story of why change must occur and the value offered by an effective interviewing process implemented companywide. Create this dissatisfaction, and then inspire others by looking at what would happen if a new process were in place. Convince them that things can be better and that the Behavior-Based Interviewing process is the way to achieve this goal.

If you are the chief champion and implementation leader, it will be your job to interact with other company leaders, both within Human Resources and elsewhere in the company, to sell the compelling aspects of your business case based on quantifiable evidence and promised results. Your business case should quantify the cost of the current reality, then go on to show the impact on the business of doing a better job of interviewing. If executive management and hiring managers understand the business reasons for making a significant change in the way they interview and select candidates, they will also see the new interviewing program as necessary because it affects the organization's livelihood.

Obtain the Support of Leaders and Champions

Change is best carried out as a team effort, with many champions and key stakeholders strategically positioned throughout the organization, and with top-level executive support in every department in which hiring occurs. Those who are committed to the change effort and who have the authority to drive change should be put in place.

There is usually one designated "champion" for a major change process. This might be you—in that case, you will have to be visionary, persuasive, and consistent in communicating the need for change and the value of the new program. You will want to recruit other leaders and champions, perhaps a task force, who will use their influence and persistence and smart communication efforts to build support for the new approach. Some best practices in this area include the following:

- Create a task force that's sold on the effort, and ensure that each member of the task force has a key role and set of tasks. The team gets the word out for its assigned departments, ensures that every hiring manager has been trained, serves as a resource, leads ongoing refresher training and coaching, and holds managers in each area of responsibility accountable for their hiring practices. The task force should have a reporting structure so that a member who leaves or is reassigned can be replaced easily and efficiently. Members of the task force are the experts on Behavior-Based Interviewing and have the skills and resources to help hiring managers at any stage of the process.

- Maintain the visible presence of executive support before, during, and after everyone starts using Behavior-Based Interview questions to select new employees. Executive presence should be consistent and can be in the form of written communications and success stories that reinforce the reason for the change. Executives should visit the training sessions, for example, and talk about why they believe in this process and how it ties to the company mission. If the vice president of sales shows up at training sessions for managers involved in hiring sales representatives, they will know that this is important.

- Leaders should meet with all the hiring managers to fully explain the reasons for the change, the importance of the implementation effort, how it will initially be carried out, and where managers can go for additional information and resources.

- Leaders must practice what they preach so that the change effort will have dramatic and positive results. Leaders validate the process, help build consensus, and foster overall acceptance by sharing their belief and conviction in Behavior-Based Interviewing by using it themselves. The old-fashioned way is to "do as I say, not as I do." If there is a disconnect at the top and executives aren't using Behavior-Based Interviewing or don't even know about it, the effort will falter and the methods taught will stop being used.

Showstopper: Inconsistent Application of Behavior-Based Interviewing Techniques

How can you be sure that hiring managers are using the new program once it has been implemented? Buy-in, thorough training, ongoing communication, and encouragement are all important. But here are some ways you can bring even recalcitrant managers into the fold.

- Mandate the change—don't allow managers to be involved in interviewing at all unless they have gone through the training process.
- Hold managers accountable for the quality of new hires and employee retention—and back up this accountability with performance incentives for those who excel.
- Be prepared for every excuse in the book when managers resist the training or the program: *I'm too busy. I know how to interview. I'll pick up the essentials from someone else.* Reiterate the program's value and benefits, its top-down company implementation, and its place in evaluating a manager's performance. With persistent communication, encouragement, and a mandate from the top, you should be able to bring even the most resistant manager on board.
- Publish success stories and results from all areas of the company. Create a competitive environment in which managers will want to outdo each other in making great hires. Make sure they understand how important Behavior-Based Interviewing is in achieving this result.
- Persuade a top executive to serve as the chief champion of the program.

Communicate and Sell

The next step is to begin communicating with and educating your target audience—everyone involved in hiring—about this new effort that will be taking place. Grab the attention of your audience and spread the word, using the methods that work best in your own company. Your marketing, internal communications, and human resources departments can get involved and develop a customized communications plan to fit the needs of your program. Communications tools might include posters, brochures, newsletter articles, memos and emails, conference calls, and in-person meetings. Some companies really get into the spirit of the change by creating a brand, logo, and theme for the new program.

When communicating the information about this program, share the reasons behind the change, how the change will occur, what to do to participate, and what the requirements are. Include executive backing and commitment, benefits, best practices, and success stories in all of your communications.

Frequent communication and education is the best way to deal with and even avert resistance. Keep your messages top of mind by consistent and constant reminders. Let your target audience know what the program is about and why it is important to them. So that they understand the motivation behind the change, share with them a piece of the business case and help them understand that the goal is to recruit the highest-quality people. Some people are motivated by what's also important to their superiors, so it's important to keep executive backing visible. Use the communications tactics that work best in your company and, if possible, integrate them into other initiatives so that the Behavior-Based Interviewing message isn't a standalone effort.

Provide workshops and training courses to those who have already bought into Behavior-Based Interviewing, and have them help promote it and spread the word about it. This group more than likely will comprise your Human Resources team, particularly your hiring and recruiting professionals. Demonstrate results, talk about what's been successful, show a return on investment, and promote the program to get other departments asking about it. Widely communicate the need for change, what's being done about it, and what's been working well. If done right, the communications plan should generate excitement. To be sure that the process is taken seriously, link the effort to the goals, mission, and values of the organization.

Create Corporate Standards and Common Materials

Before you can introduce a Behavior-Based Interviewing program to managers at your company, you must have on hand the materials that they will need to implement the program for each job opening. To encourage widespread adoption, make the process as easy for them as possible.

Develop Centralized Core Competencies and Interview Questions

- Starting with Human Resources, tap your Behavior-Based Interviewing leaders team to create a centralized, corporate competency

profile and defined job competency profiles for the most frequently
filled jobs. The more recognizable these competencies are and the
more integrated they are into the corporation mission and other
areas of the business, such as performance management and succession planning, the greater success you will have.

- From these competency profiles, develop questions to be used by
  the hiring managers. Use the questions in Chapter 4, either word
  for word or as a guideline for developing unique questions for
  your company and its culture.

- Require hiring managers to interview to the defined competencies,
  and encourage them to utilize the questions that are provided. At
  the very least, have a team of in-house experts craft questions for
  managers on an as-needed basis.

Prepare Interview Guides for Hiring Managers

A hiring manager will apply the methods of Behavior-Based Interviewing better if she is provided with actual Interview Guides containing
preplanned questions. In your program's early stages, it is a good idea to
review the Interview Guides after a session to be sure they are being
used and to ensure consistency and good note taking. You might also
wish to include facilitators (from your Behavior-Based Interviewing
leaders team) in the post interview decision-making meetings, at least
during the critical first months that the new program is in place.

Train and Follow Up

The most important step in implementing a new interviewing process is
actually training people in how to do it. When they complete the training,
participants should know how to interview using the new Behavior-Based
guidelines. Good training will teach them to value this new method, so
that they become advocates for it. We recommend that training be
mandated, whether it is part of new manager orientation training or an
overall new program rolled out to all managers, and that you require all
managers to complete the training before they are allowed to participate
in interviewing and hiring.

You will want to develop a training program that addresses the specific needs of your company. Here is a step-by-step plan that you can
use as a blueprint.

Do Your Research

Start by talking to a cross section of hiring managers to gain a clear picture of the challenges they face when they are hiring new employees. Tell them that if they are going to spend a few hours or days of their time, you want to make sure they get methods and tools that they can implement immediately. You can't do that without their valuable input.

Depending on the size of your organization, the number of hiring managers, and the method that is the norm at your company, you can use a questionnaire, one-on-one meetings, or small focus groups to gather this information. Here are some questions you might ask:

- What is your current hiring process from start to finish?
- What works and what doesn't?
- What role does Human Resources play? What about recruiters?
- What is your involvement?
- Tell me about an actual interview.
- How can we provide the greatest value to you in these new training programs? What deliverables do you expect, and how can we make the program worth your time?

The key is to be informed about your company's hiring process in all areas. The more tightly you can weave the training program and the Behavior-Based Interviewing process into the company fabric, the more buy-in you'll obtain and the greater your chances of success.

Create a Structure

Use the data that you collected from your interviews and questionnaires to design and structure the training program. Begin by determining how many and which people you will train, the groupings that make sense, and the most efficient ways to deliver training to these groups. Most managers want the information as quickly as possible so that they can get back to their business at hand. Fast and effective don't always go hand and hand, though, so work on balancing the key learning objectives with what's acceptable in your organization to make training stick. For example, pulling managers out for an entire week of training may not be the best strategy if their business operations will suffer, and managers typically don't like lengthy programs. Establish the length of and criteria for the program, group size, number of sessions, prework, the program itself, and follow-up activities, and begin to plan a pilot. Develop learning objectives and have the instructional materials developed to enable participants to achieve those objectives.

These guidelines and recommendations will help as you develop your program:

- Develop preclass reading materials and exercises to give participants a general understanding of the principles of Behavior-Based Interviewing.
- Limit the size of the training group to ensure high levels of interaction.
- Vary the class format. Typical components include lectures, case studies, exercises, question-and-answer sessions, group discussions, and, most importantly, practice sessions to help participants gain confidence and expertise in Behavior-Based Interviewing.
- These practice sessions will be a key part of your training program. Consider these ideas:
  - Have participants conduct actual interviews—a good format is a group of three, with an interviewer, a candidate, and a recorder/observer who can critique and provide feedback. Switch roles until all group members have played all three parts.
  - Videotape the interview practice sessions. This is particularly valuable in small groups or one-on-one, where a facilitator can review the session and provide instant feedback. Video is a very powerful tool because it provides direct evidence of someone's interviewing skills, and most hiring managers want to improve their technique.
  - Consider inviting actors, temporary workers, or college students to pose as real candidates and participate in the practice sessions. It will be helpful to have these individuals go through three or four rounds of interviews, as if they were interviewing for a real job at your company, so that you can practice the group rating component of Behavior-Based candidate selection.
  - Whether or not you use videotape, include a "debriefing" session after each practice interview. Talk about what worked well and what didn't, what the participants learned, and how they can improve their interviewing technique. Resolve any stumbling blocks or problems, and give them another opportunity to try out their new skills.

- Have participants practice note taking using an Interview Guide. You can test how well they grasp the concept of complete SAR stories by providing statements and asking participants whether the statements or answers are behavioral and complete and, if not, what probes should be used to get the full situation, action, and results. (At the end of Chapter 2 is an exercise you can use that tests knowledge of the types of interview questions.)
- Incorporate Rating Sheets into the practice sessions. Have participants fill these out, identify any missing, whole, or partial SAR statements, and discuss and defend their ratings with others who interviewed the same candidate. The more you practice this part of the training, the better equipped your managers will be to gather complete information and to evaluate candidates based on complete SAR statements.
- Don't let managers off the hook. Have training and makeup training sessions scheduled on a regular basis, and consider developing self-study materials for independent learning. It is important to reinforce self-study with practice and review sessions that prove that the methods have been learned.

Provide Follow-Up

Postclassroom work is as critical as the actual training day. Cognitive and technical learning occurs in the classroom, but skills building occurs in practice sessions, on the job during actual interviews, and in follow-up coaching. Be prepared to reinforce and extend the learning process with follow-up coaching, post training activities, and refresher programs. Here are some methods you can use:

- Schedule reviews and refresher training quarterly, or within the time frame that works best for your company.
- Develop resource, refresher, and self-study materials that managers can use to address problems that come up when they are using the new system.
- Create a resource list of Behavior-Based Interviewing champions for every department, and make sure each manager knows whom to call if there is a problem.

Training is a long-term investment in your people, your company, and your company's future and strategic direction, and you don't want the knowledge that has been learned to fizzle out. Integrate your refresher programs into the initial implementation strategy and schedule so that they don't get lost in the excitement of the new program or the relief of getting it off the ground.

Measure and Evaluate

Why is it important to evaluate and measure? Because you can kill an incredibly great concept with a few bad experiences that give it a bad name. There's no point in organizing an effort and putting a lot of time and resources behind it unless it is done right and shows a return on investment. Make a commitment to a solid and meaningful evaluation to determine whether your program really is making a difference. If there is no feedback, two things may occur: First, people will assume that the program has lost its urgency and importance, and consequently will be less committed to implementing it and, second, because of the "no news is good news" tendency to think that everything is going well, issues that need attention will not be dealt with.

- *Evaluate training sessions.* Ask participants what was most helpful to them during the session. Written evaluations should be ongoing and should be handed out at the end of each training module. Listen, learn, and get feedback on how the program could be changed or modified. Get participants to talk during the session about what they will do differently as a result of this class.
- *Evaluate training effectiveness.* Go beyond the "feel-good" data that say that the classroom training sessions were enjoyable and helpful. After some time has passed, get practical feedback from the participants in terms of what stood out, what needs improvement, what they have implemented, where they are having difficulty, and what skills they have already put to the test.
- *Evaluate the interviewing process.* Review used Interview Guides and notes to see whether the process was followed consistently. Survey new hires to see if they were asked Behavior-Based questions and what they thought of the hiring process.
- *Measure results over time.* Use concrete, quantifiable scales to measure the success of the new program, and develop a strategy and a regular schedule for measuring data. Use the criteria defined in

your original business case—quality of employee reviews, percentage of employee turnover, sales results, and customer satisfaction scores, for example—as key measures of the success of your program.

Measuring successes and results is a way to convince a broader audience that this new method of interviewing really is working. It helps build momentum, sustain enthusiasm, and ensure a successful program that will go on to win the test of time. You need to show a return on investment to justify the expense and time invested in the new program—for

Showstopper: Inconclusive Performance/Undocumented Results

What happens if your Behavior-Based Interviewing program does not produce the outcomes you expected? Consider these options if you are not showing a clear trend of improvement in your hiring results:

- Be sure you have accurately tracked all costs resulting from a bad hire. Reanalyze company performance before and after implementing Behavior-Based Interviewing.
- Survey hiring managers to find out what's working with the new system, where they're having problems, and if they're really using the system as they should. Cross-check these manager reports by surveying new employees concerning their experiences with the Behavior-Based Interviewing process.
- Invigorate your training programs and add refresher courses.
- Review your core competencies and sample questions to be sure that you have hit on the right mix of questions to assess technical skills and knowledge, behaviors/performance skills, and job and company fit.
- Seek anecdotal evidence. Ask Human Resources and hiring managers about their experiences using Behavior-Based Interviewing. Do they like it? Do they instinctively feel that it results in better hires? Don't give up trying to produce hard evidence, but do take anecdotal tales into account when evaluating the success of your program.
- Be sure all the other pieces of your hiring practices are fostering good results. Review the sections on résumé screening, telephone screening, and reference checking in Chapter 9.

planning, implementation, materials, and training. Quantify the value of your new program and you will build ongoing commitment all across the organization.

Other Tips and Strategies

The following suggestions will help you troubleshoot and resolve any additional roadblocks you may encounter as you implement and execute Behavior-Based Interviewing at your company.

- *Align your strategy with your culture.* Adopt a rollout and implementation strategy that fits the culture of your company. Review other successful company initiatives—what worked, what didn't work, and what strategy and tactics were most successful in gaining and sustaining momentum for the change initiative.
- *Start small.* You want your effort to be successful, so start out with a pilot program. Involve individuals who are most likely to do well, embrace the effort, spread the word, and create short-term successes that will temper the skeptics.
- *Sustain success.* Your implementation strategy must be executed in a sustainable way and ingrained in your organization. This is necessary so that participants won't be tempted to take shortcuts or revert to using gut feeling when making important hiring decisions. To make your effort stick, consider building a refresher course program, developing greater numbers of in-house experts (those individuals who act as resources for all other hiring managers), soliciting regular feedback from candidates and hiring managers, mandating the change, and measuring the quality of new hires by holding managers accountable.
- *Don't do everything yourself.* To be successful, you need a lot of arms and legs and resources to help you get this effort off the ground and to sustain momentum and excitement. Don't reinvent the wheel. Use the resources we've provided in this book, beginning with the forms in Appendix 2. Call on your in-house experts in the areas of training, marketing, and human resources. You might also want to bring in outside consultants who are experts in the field of Behavior-Based Interviewing. They can help you develop an effective strategy and can take on several of the steps

outlined in this chapter and in Chapter 3. A resource list of outside consultants can be found in Appendix 1.

Behavior-Based Interviewing Program Checklist

Use the following checklist to determine if the odds on having a successful companywide implementation are in your favor. *All* of these items are critical components in the success of your program. If you cannot check "yes" for each, take a step back, review the relevant sections of this chapter, and address the missing components so that your program will launch with a roar and deliver benefits to your company far into the future.

___ Change Effectiveness—I've identified the barriers to change in my organization, reviewed our history of effective change initiatives, and identified their success factors. My organization is comfortable and ready for change.

___ Vision Defined—A clear vision of this initiative has been developed and its benefits defined.

___ Stakeholders Identified—Key stakeholders, leaders, and champions who "own" this business initiative and will drive and support it have been identified.

___ Communications Plan—My task force is clear about the initiative, and a targeted communications plan has been developed to educate, create buy-in, and provide training schedules and resources. The messages will be frequent and sustained.

___ Materials—We understand the common materials that we need to create, and we have established a plan and a team for their development.

___ Training Program—We are prepared to develop and roll out a comprehensive training program for our new initiative. We have allocated the resources and have developed at least a rough framework for the training program.

___ Evaluation—An evaluation plan has been established for the training programs and the actual interviewing process.

___ Maintaining Success—There is a plan to address hiring managers' needs after implementation and to sustain success.

CHAPTER

Final Thoughts and Ideas

Ideas must work through the brains and the arms of good and brave men, or they are no better than dreams.

—Ralph Waldo Emerson

As WE NEAR THE end of our book, we hope you are energized, informed, and eager to move forward with your Behavior-Based Interviewing program. We've given you a lot of information—both theory and practical hands-on application—that will equip you to launch a Behavior-Based Interviewing program at your company. There's no doubt that this undertaking will require a commitment of time, energy, and company resources. Not only that, it demands champions and leaders who will carry the flag throughout the entire planning and implementation process and on into the program's daily use within your company.

But first let's look at your program from the perspective of several months or years after implementation. After enjoying the first flush of satisfaction from orchestrating a companywide change, you will want to put systems in place to sustain its success.

Review Your Process from Time to Time

As described in Chapter 8, systems for evaluating and measuring results are an essential part of the program and will enable you to prove the business case you presented when you launched the program. More specifically, it is a good idea to create a periodic review procedure for your hiring processes under the new Behavior-Based Interviewing program. With hiring managers, representatives from Human Resources, and other members of your Behavior-Based Interviewing leaders team, ask these questions:

- Are we using enough interviewers to gather a complete picture of each candidate from diverse perspectives?
- Are we using *too many* interviewers, making unnecessary work for our busy employees?
- Does the interview process take too long? If so, how can we streamline it?
- Is the interview process rushed? If so, how can we allow sufficient time without losing efficiency?
- Do we follow the process from start to finish? If steps are skipped, where does this happen and why? How can we avoid this in future? Or, are the skipped steps truly an essential part of the process? If not, revise the system.
- Does everyone involved in the process, including the candidates, express positive feelings about it? If not, do we have a system for looking into these less-than-positive experiences?
- Does the process run smoothly? If there are stumbling blocks, where do they occur? Are they one-time or persistent problems? What can we do about them?
- Do we find the best candidate for each position?
- What could we do differently? How can we make our process even better?

The information you gather from these review sessions will be tremendously valuable for keeping your Behavior-Based Interviewing system in tune with the needs and behaviors at your company. These sessions also reinforce the benefits of the system and will reinspire your team of leaders and champions, thereby keeping Behavior-Based

Interviewing an integral part of your company culture and well-knit into daily behaviors.

Review Other Pieces of the Hiring Puzzle

Behavior-Based Interviewing promotes good hires. Yet there are other elements of the hiring process that can have a big impact on the people you select for interviews and how you narrow down and make a final choice from a slate of candidates.

Résumé Screening

Be sure that the staff members who are screening résumés are qualified and trained for this important task. You don't want to waste interviewers' time with unqualified candidates, but neither do you want to overlook excellent candidates whose résumés do not do them justice. Use the Job Competency Charts (see Chapter 3) created for each open position to define screening criteria that match the needs for the specific job. Train screeners to look for more than easy-to-identify qualifications such as a college degree or professional certification. They should also look for evidence of core competencies in the experience and achievements included in the résumé. Here's an example: For the marketing manager example in Chapter 3, we defined "Sales" as a key competency area and specifically identified "two years in direct sales, achieving 100 percent of quota" as a required performance action. Because not every résumé will contain this information in precisely those terms, here are some things your résumé screeners can look for that would indicate a high likelihood of the candidate's meeting this requirement:

- Sales awards
- President's Club or other designation for high achievers
- Sales training responsibilities (usually it is the most successful salespeople who are chosen for this role)
- Advancement from one sales position to a higher-level position or select account base

We recommend a checklist format that screeners can use to evaluate each résumé for key competencies, as well as to identify "red flags" that should be called to the interviewer's attention. These items should be clarified, usually in a telephone screen before the individual is invited in. Examples include

- Gaps in employment
- Short-term employment (especially a history of repeated short-term jobs)
- Lack of advancement (an extended length of time in one position or repeated employment with the same job title)
- Lack of a degree or other educational credentials, where these qualifications are preferred but are not a genuine job requirement
- Experience in a different industry or serving different customers
- A functional résumé style that disguises years of employment and career chronology

"Red flag" items deserve further investigation but should not automatically disqualify a candidate. As résumé writers, we have daily proof that many individuals do a poor job of writing their own résumés. When they are interviewed by a professional who can draw out their expertise, most are able to share impressive results, powerful SAR stories, and strong qualifications. Yet many don't get the opportunity to share their expertise because their résumés do a poor job of representing them to hiring authorities. Because you are in the business of finding good people for your company, you should train your screeners to do their utmost to screen candidates *into* rather than *out of* the selection process. Of course you must whittle down a large stack of résumés to manageable size, but you will increase your qualified candidate pool if you give applicants a bit of the benefit of the doubt on initial screening. Use telephone screens to further refine the initial pool before selecting candidates for interviews.

Testing and Assessments

At some companies, formal testing and assessments are included in the candidate-selection process. There is a science to these kinds of tests; it is a separate field of study, and there are highly qualified experts who can help you should you choose to add these to your hiring tools. We recommend that before moving forward, you carefully assess your hiring results to identify any gaps in knowledge. This will enable you to introduce the testing instruments that will give you the information you need to make better hiring decisions.

There are several ways to integrate testing and assessments into your overall hiring process, including the following:

- Introduce testing and assessments during the screening phase to keep interviewers from talking to the wrong people during the interviewing stage.
- Administer assessments to successful employees in the same job you are hiring for to identify common success factors to interview for.
- Perform testing on team members when a job opening occurs to identify team productivity gaps that could be solved by a new hire who could fill those gaps.
- Assimilate testing into your company by using the results to further develop new hires to become productive team members and to have strong employee-manager relationships.

There are many benefits to integrating testing into your hiring process. Testing allows you to learn things about a candidate that are not subjectively detectable. For example, you will know if a candidate is capable of closing sales, what corporate culture he will perform best in, what his management style is, and how he prefers to learn. Along with Behavior-Based Interviewing, testing and assessments provide you with a more complete picture so that you can make the right hiring decision.

Be certain that you follow fair-hiring guidelines in administering any tests or assessments. As discussed in Chapter 6, you must administer tests equitably—to *all* candidates who have reached the same stage of a hiring process.

Reference Checking

Checking candidates' references should be an integral part of your hiring process. You will easily uncover any fabricated credentials or misstated work history, but beyond that, you can gain valuable insights into how the candidate performed when dealing with challenges that are similar to what she will face at your company.

When checking references, you may initially run into a brick wall because many companies restrict their official reference verification to dates of employment and possibly salary information. These sources should not be ignored, because you will want to cross-check starting and ending dates with the information supplied by the candidate. But you will not get the information you're looking for: how the candidate performed on the job. For that you will need to go beyond the human resources departments of past employers. Ask your candidates for names and contact information for their references. If they come up with only the official sources, press them for the names of people they worked with in the past, peers and subordinates as well as supervisors, or perhaps their customers or vendors. From that point, a good way to expand your list is to ask each reference you speak with for the name of another person who might be able to provide some insight into the candidate's behaviors and motivations.

You can use Behavior-Based questions as a valuable tool when speaking with references. Recall the story of TD Madison and Associates in Chapter 5. Behavior-Based questions let them go beyond surface recommendations to give specific evidence of how candidates behaved in the past. Here are a few examples:

- Give me an example of how Tonya reacts when her work is criticized.
- Tell me about a time when Chris had to implement an unpopular policy.
- Share a story about Luis that illustrates his problem-solving skills.
- What incidents come to mind when you think about Dale's leadership style?

Your reference checks should support the evidence you've gained during your interview process; if they do not, you will want to look very closely at that candidate to find out why there is this discrepancy. Thorough reference checks will help you make distinctions between two or more well-qualified candidates.

From start to finish to follow-up, you're now ready to implement Behavior-Based Interviewing at your company. The information, tools, and resources we've provided will guide you from the initial development, championing, and implementation through active use and ongoing refinement of your program. Your investment will be rewarded by right-fit people who deliver top performance and great results for your company. With Behavior-Based Interviewing as your primary tool, you can begin building an organization of top performers, one hire at a time.

Consultants and Expert Resources for Behavior-Based Interviewing

IN THIS SECTION we provide some resources that can lift your load: information on consulting companies that are experts in the planning, development, and implementation of Behavior-Based Interviewing programs.

If your staff resources are limited or your organization isn't very large, you may find it difficult to allocate the necessary time and effort to planning and implementing a Behavior-Based Interviewing program company-wide. We have compiled information on firms that specialize in this process. We are not endorsing any of these companies, but merely identifying them as resources for you to consider. When evaluating a firm, you should subject it to a rigorous investigation to be certain that it is a good fit for your company and its needs. Here are some questions you might ask:

- How many Behavior-Based Interviewing programs have you implemented?
- Describe the size, industry, and culture of the companies at which you have done this work.
- What was the status of each company's program 6 months, 1 year, and 3 years after implementation?

- What challenges did you encounter? How did you resolve them?
- Looking back at programs that were not as successful as you would have liked, what could you have done differently?
- What is the expertise of your staff?
- Describe the process of working with us. What activities and what timeline do you envision for each step?
- Who will be our main point of contact? What is that person's expertise and experience? How long has he or she been with your firm? What resources do we have if we experience difficulty with that person?
- What is your guarantee?
- How long after implementation will you continue to work with us?
- What are your fees? How do you calculate your fees? For those fees, what services and support will we receive?
- Please supply the names of four to six references at companies where you have implemented similar programs.

The companies that follow are broken down by the size of the organization—*not* the size of the companies it serves. The descriptions were compiled from information provided by each firm in response to a standard questionnaire.

400 to 1000 Employees

Development Dimensions International (DDI)

1225 Washington Pike
Bridgeville, PA 15017
Tel.: 412-257-0700
Email: info@ddiworld.com
Web site: www.ddiworld.com

What this company offers: *Since 1970 DDI has helped clients worldwide achieve superior business results by building engaged, high-performing workforces by selecting, developing, and retaining extraordinary people. We specialize in identifying and developing leaders and helping you hire better people faster. What sets DDI apart is realization—we have a passion for client success.*

Kenexa
650 E. Swedesford Road
Wayne, PA 19087
Tel.: 800-391-9557
Email: Sarah.Teten@kenexa.com
Web site: www.kenexa.com

What this company offers: *Founded in 1987, Kenexa provides comprehensive talent management solutions integrating software and services for talent acquisition and performance management. Kenexa helps organizations improve and align their talent, better manage the complete employee life cycle, increase business performance, and reduce costs. Kenexa's clients are diverse in size and industries and include more than 100 of the Fortune 500 and half of the Dow 30.*

Novations Group, Inc.
5255 N. Edgewood Drive, Suite 125
Provo, UT 84604
Tel.: 801-375-7525
Email: sdcinfo@novations.com
Web site: www.novations.com

What this company offers: *Novations' Selection, Development, and Communication Division helps organizations worldwide achieve superior business results by improving employee contribution at all levels—from new hires to senior executives. Based on Novations' Four Stages of Contribution framework, we provide proven training, consulting, and measurement solutions in the areas of selection, development, and communication. Nationwide coverage with offices in Utah, Boston, New York, and San Francisco.*

Personnel Decisions International (PDI)
2000 Plaza VII Tower, 45 South Seventh Street
Minneapolis, MN 55402
Tel.: 800-633-4410
Web site: www.personneldecisions.com

What this company offers: *PDI is a global consulting firm offering standard and customized solutions backed by research and proven methodology that improve business results. PDI's expertise includes assessment, performance modeling, staffing, training, development, coaching, 360-degree feedback, career management, and organizational solutions. PDI has offices throughout Asia, Australia, Europe, and North America.*

Over 85 Employees

Manchester, Inc.

255 State Street, 5th Floor

Boston MA 02109

Tel.: 617-523-9190

Email: Ted.Bililies@ManchesterUS.com

Web site: www.manchesterusa.com

What this company offers: *Manchester can help you interview applicants effectively by preparing interview questions, identifying elements of a successful interview, recognizing the importance and limits of an interview, distinguishing consequences of poor interviewing, designing a tailored interview, and making sure you are aware of the guidelines differentiating lawful from unlawful questions. Manchester provides career transition, executive development, and performance management solutions in over 150 U.S. cities as well as more than 30 countries around the world.*

Talent Plus

5220 South 16th Street

Lincoln, NE 68512

Tel.: 402-489-2000 or 1-800-VARSITY

Email: ckoukol@talentplus.com

Web site: www.talentplus.com

What this company offers: *Taking an aptitude-based approach to selection, Talent Plus focuses on identifying people who have the behavioral and cognitive precursors (thoughts, feelings, and behaviors) to be successful at a job after they have received the appropriate training for it—even if they haven't had the opportunity to do that job before. Our empirically validated, structured interviews help clients select, retain, and develop people who have talents similar to those found in the people performing with excellence in that client's business today. Our selection instruments are available in 20 languages and may be administered in a person-to-person or Web-based format.*

Over 20 Associates

The Adler Group

17852 17th St., #209

Tustin, CA 92780

Tel.: 714-573-1820

Email: info@adlerconcepts.com (Lou Adler)
Web site: www.adlerconcepts.com

What this company offers: *Since 1988 The Adler Group has trained over 20,000 hiring managers and recruiters across the United States, Canada, and Europe in performance-based hiring. This is a form of behavioral event interviewing that focuses on determining what behaviors candidates used to achieve major accomplishments. These major accomplishments are then compared to the accomplishments required for on-the-job success. Research has shown that this approach increases an interviewer's ability to assess both competency and motivation for the job.*

AIRS

58 Fogg Farm Road
White River Junction, VT 05001
Tel.: 800-466-4010
Email: sales@airsdirectory.com
Web site: www.airsdirectory.com

What this company offers: *AIRS offers seminars and workshops that span the e-recruitment landscape. We are the leading innovator and premium brand in our marketplace, with more than 2000 public seminars and corporate training sessions under our belt and 25,000 alumni, including a high percentage of the Fortune and Global 500. Training is available in the United States and Canada; tools are available internationally.*

APT, Inc.

1120 Post Road, 2nd Floor
Darien, CT 06820
Tel.: 203-655-7779
Email: info@appliedpsych.com
Web site: www.appliedpsych.com

What this company offers: *APT is a full-service, national human resource consulting firm with offices in the New York, Seattle, Atlanta, and San Jose metropolitan areas. Owned and staffed by industrial/organizational psychologists, APT's areas of expertise include Behavior-Based Interviewing as part of the job analysis process. These interviews are used as part of candidate test development and the validation of these tests. Additional expertise: Assessment/360-Degree Feedback; Selection; HR Process Audits; Staffing for Organizational Change; Performance Development and Management; Organizational Surveys; and Test Scoring.*

The Assessment and Development Group International Inc. (ADGI)

25 Chinquapin Road, P.O. Box 5317
Pinehurst, NC 28374
1370 Don Mills Road, Suite 300
Toronto, Ontario M3B 3N7
Tel.: 910-295-3838 (Pinehurst); 416-445-9551 (Toronto)
Email: fgump@2oms.com
Web site: www.2oms.com

What this company offers: *ADGI provides three interviewing services to clients. Initially we do job behavioral profiling, including the creation of competencies and behavioral modeling to identify personalities most compatible with the competencies. We develop company- and job-specific behavioral simulations based upon job activities and competencies, and offer training on both behavioral interviewing and selection. The training includes both the development and use of behaviorally based questions. Our assessment and training services are available throughout the United States and Canada, both directly from ADGI and indirectly through associated consultants.*

Cambria Consulting, Inc.

One Bowdoin Square
Boston, MA 02114
Tel.: 617-523-7500
Email: gklemp@cambriaconsulting.com
Web site: www.cambriaconsulting.com

What this company offers: *Cambria Consulting offers customized behavioral interviewing solutions for hiring and assessing people in technical, professional, managerial, and executive positions. The principals of Cambria Consulting were among the first to champion the use of behavioral interviewing over 30 years ago. We offer training in Cambria's Critical Behavior Interview (CBI) technique as well as total recruiting, selection, and executive assessment strategies for leading-edge North American companies with global reach.*

Jeanneret & Associates, Inc.

601 Jefferson, Suite 3900
Houston, TX 77002
Tel.: 713-650-6535
Email: dick@jeanneret.com
Web site: www.jeanneret.com

What this company offers: *We offer the design and implementation of Behavior-Based Interviewing instruments nationwide that comprise a component of candidate selection or promotion procedures. Design includes the preparation of Behavior-Based questions using job-relevant resources and the development of scoring protocols. Implementation includes training in the use of Behavior-Based Interviewing procedures, interview process strategies (single interviewer, interview panels, on-line administration), scoring, and data retention.*

Under 20 Associates

Action Insight, Inc.

430 Columbine Avenue
Broomfield, CO 80020
Tel.: 303-439-2001
Email: steve@actioninsight.com
Web site: www.actioninsight.com

What this company offers: *Action Insight was established in 1997 to provide leading-edge training and software for Behavioral-Based systems for the selection and retention of talent. Action Insight's founder Stephen Moulton has worked with and refined behavioral competencies and the interview process for over 25 years in such industries as Aerospace, Consumer Products, Medical Products and Services, Capital Equipment, Telecommunications, and Insurance.*

Advanced HR Solutions, Inc.

10127 Northwestern Ave.
Franksville, WI 53126
Tel.: 262-909-4370
Email: vivian@advancedhrsolutions.com
Web site: www.advancedhrsolutions.com

What this company offers: *Advanced HR Solutions is highly skilled in developing Behavior-Based Interviews for a variety of technical and managerial-level positions, as well as in interpreting the responses to such interviews. We utilize Behavior-Based Interviews as one of our primary selection tools in recruiting and executive search assignments that require the selection of qualified individuals for difficult-to-fill and managerial/executive-level positions. We specialize in servicing the utility and manufacturing industries in the Midwest and have done a number of projects for not-for-profit agencies.*

Behavior Description Technologies (BDT)
3500 Boxwood Drive
Grapevine, TX 76051
Tel.: 800-666-8681
Web site: www.bdt.net

What this company offers: *BDT is led by the scientist whose research, reported in the* Journal of Applied Psychology *and elsewhere, paved the way for the popularity of Behavior-Based Interviewing, and whose book* Behavior Description Interviewing: New, Accurate, Cost Effective *introduced thousands of hirers to the power of Behavior Description interviewing. Behavior Description Technologies offers instructor-led interviewer training, supported by workbooks and a video, and offers train-the-trainer instruction with a detailed Leader's Guide. We offer computer-assisted skills coaching via BDCoach, a downloadable skills assessment tool that generates a coaching session guide. BDT offers the only online, interactive behavioral interviewing process (called E.ssessor) that is more consistent, easier to administer, and easier for hiring managers to use. BDT services clients primarily in North America, with an associate network in Europe and Australia.*

CBI Group LLC
Casho Mill Professional Center, Suite 8
1501 Casho Mill Road
Newark, DE 19711
Tel.: 877-746-8450-13
Web site: www.thecbigroup.com

What this company offers: *The staffing team of CBI Group has been successfully practicing Behavioral-Based Interviewing for more than 10 years. Team members are trained on how to lead an applicant through situations to discover how individuals react when they are comfortable and uncomfortable. This has resulted not only in better hires for clients, but better core team member hires for CBI Group. We work primarily in the Mid-Atlantic region.*

Cluff & Associates
12554 Cross Country Lane
Reston, VA 20191
Tel.: 703-689-3458 or 800-890-2795
Email: gary@cluffassociates.com
Web site: www.cluffassociates.com

What this company offers: *We create and deliver throughout the United States a training program of either one- or two-day duration customized to include an organization-specific employment process, selection profile, and interview guide/evaluation form.*

Davidson's Consulting a.k.a. Alan D. Davidson's, Ph.D. Incorporated
4660 La Jolla Village Drive
San Diego, CA 92122-4660
Tel.: 858-535-8033
Email: amber@alandavidsonconsulting.com
Web site: www.alandavidsonconsulting.com

What this company offers: *Dr. Davidson divides his professional time among executive assessment, speaking, and training engagements and management consultation. He has evaluated thousands of candidates in his over 20 years of practice. His assessment candidates have included, but are not limited to, those applying for positions in manufacturing, retail, banking, engineering, advertising, law enforcement, aviation, sales, and management.*

Dubois & Associates
P.O. Box 10340
Rockville, MD 20849-0340
Tel.: 301-762-5026
Email: duboisassociates@yahoo.com

What this company offers: *David Dubois and his associates are well published and are internationally recognized for their expertise in the design, development, and application of competency-based human resource management practices, including the use of competency-based employee recruitment and selection practices. They offer short-term consulting services and a one-day workshop targeted to help any size organization take advantage of the benefits derived from using competency-based employee recruitment and selection practices.*

EDA Human Resource Services
1157 Westlake Blvd.
Naples, FL 34103
Tel.: 239-262-3318
Email: edahrsvcs@aol.com
Web site: www.edahr.com

What this company offers: *EDA Human Resource Services drafts behavioral interview guides by establishing core competencies and writes questions designed to determine whether the candidate can meet them. We also train those who conduct the interview in how to determine criteria, write the questions, and conduct the interview. Also discussed is how to evaluate the ability of the applicant to meet the criteria.*

The Executive Planning Group
214 Senate Ave., Suite 303
Camp Hill, PA 17011
Tel.: 717-763-7365
Email: dmgreenwd@aol.com
Web site: www.EPGservices.com

What this company offers: *Our focus is on assessment, selection, and development of talent in the workplace. Behavior-Based Interviewing is a specific technique we use for these purposes. The design of such interviews, their administration, and the analysis of the data collected from such interviews comprise much of our work.*

GENESYS Management Company, LLC
4105 S.E. Wisconsin Avenue
Topeka, KS 66609
Tel.: 785-633-2045
Email: genesysmanagement@cox.net
Web site: Genesysmanagement.com

What this company offers: *The GENESYS Management Company, LLC, can assist you in finding the best people to join your business by offering advice for recruitment advertising; preparing job analysis, job descriptions, and individual position specifications; guiding you in learning behavioral selection interviews; and performing selection screening interviews or assessment centers on your behalf. We work nationally, but primarily in the Midwest.*

Hyde & Lichter, Inc.
744 North Fourth Street, Suite 625
Milwaukee, WI 53203
Tel.: 414-271-1776
Email: rbarcelona@hyde-lichter.com
Web site: www.hyde-lichter.com

What this company offers: *We provide human resource consulting services to clients nationally and internationally, with a concentration near southeastern*

Wisconsin and northern Illinois. We have developed Behavior-Based Interview processes for clients in construction services, insurance, printing and publishing services, consumer products, and in electric and gas utilities. These processes have been created for leadership, management, supervisory, professional, analytical, and craft positions. We also develop and use cognitive tests, simulation assessments, and personality inventories and integrate them with behavioral interview data as part of a reliable and valid selection process.

The Kingwood Group. Inc.
11636 Highland Road, Suite 103
Hartland, MI 48353
Tel.: 810-632-9420
Email: jack.smith@kingwoodgroup.com
Web site: www.detroit@kingwoodgroup.com

What this company offers: *The Kingwood Group has over 10 years' experience applying structured behavioral interviewing in various organizational settings. That experience includes conducting job analyses, developing and validating interviews for specific jobs or job families, training managers to develop and conduct interviews, and providing train-the-trainer courses for in-house personnel to develop and conduct interviews. Training formats include classroom and online. Kingwood's very popular InterviewRight CD is used by several companies to train managers and by over 25 universities to train students in skills needed to develop and conduct structured behavioral interviews.*

Management Psychology Group, P.C. (and eTest, a sister company)
3400 Peachtree Road, Suite 1600
Atlanta, GA 30326
Tel.: 404-237-6808
Email: hgolson@mpgpc.com
Web site: www.managementpsychology.com, www.etest.net

What this company offers: *The Management Psychology Group provides assessment interviews for selection and development. Our interviews are a whole-person interview, and we employ Behavioral Interviewing techniques, especially in covering the work history.*

Management Team Consultants, Inc.
1010 B Street, Suite 403
San Rafael, CA 94901
Tel.: 415-459-4800

Email: jim@interviewedge.com
Web site: www.interviewedge.com
Jim Kennedy, President

What this company offers: *Management Team Consultants, Inc.'s expertise is in one-day or shorter competency-based behavioral interviewing programs. We have additional expertise in techniques for interviewing today's diverse and multicultural work force. We use instructor-led training with ongoing online tools support. Certification of client trainers is available. We also offer Web-based instruction for the individual learner. Management Team Consultants has trainers in northern California, Houston, New York City, Philadelphia, and London, England.*

The Nielson Group

P.O. Box 922
Prosper, TX 75078
Tel.: 972-346-2892
Email: cnielson@nielsongroup.com
Web site: www.nielsongroup.com

What this company offers: *The Nielson Group provides hiring for fit strategies including training in Behavior-Based Interviewing techniques and assessments for identifying integrity, character, work attitudes, and behavioral style comparison to the job's behavioral requirements, motivators, and sales strategies. We provide services in the United States and Canada.*

Organizational Performance Dimensions

2621 6th Street, Suite 2
Santa Monica, CA 90405
Tel.: 310-450-8397
Email: knowack@opd.net
Web site: www.360feedback.org

What this company offers: *Organizational Performance Dimensions (OPD) specializes in personnel selection systems and validation including competency-based structured Behavioral Interviewing in the United States, Europe, and Latin America. OPD provides expertise in identifying job-relevant competencies, job analysis, design of structured behavioral interview guides, behavioral interview training, and validation.*

Partners in Performance, Inc.

1046 Tall Trees Dr.
Pittsburgh, PA 15241

Tel.: 412-221-7242

Email: lnemser@nb.net

What this company offers: *Partners in Performance, Inc., has taught thousands of human resources professionals and hiring managers in a variety of industries how to conduct a Behavioral Interview. We also develop customized tools to help interviewers make the right hire, such as customized behavioral questions and interview guides. We have provided services to clients throughout the United States and Mexico.*

Performance Strategies, Ltd.
5 Dakota Court

Suffern, NY 10901

Tel.: 845-368-1836

Email: Info@Performance-Strategies.com

Web site: www.Performance-Strategies.com

What this company offers: *We offer half-day and one day training on Behavioral Interviewing. At the end of our program, participants will be able to determine what interviewing behaviors support EEO, select three to four competencies for a job, identify the different kinds of questions used in interviewing, describe the interview process, conduct a behavioral interview, and describe how to evaluate candidates. Our services are delivered worldwide.*

R. S. Mansfield Associates
20 Lincoln Lane

Sudbury, MA 01776

Tel.: 978-443-9668

Email: Mansfield627@earthlink.net

What this company offers: *We consult on the selection process and the kinds of interviews needed: experience and education interviews, behavioral event interviews, hypothetical situations interviews, case interviews. We develop interview protocols, guides, and questions for use with specific jobs and client needs. We provide interview training and follow-up coaching throughout the United States and United Kingdom.*

Scontrino & Associates
21832 S.E. 28th Street

Sammamish, WA 90875

Tel.: 425-392-5694

Email: mpeterscontrino@aol.com

Web site: www.scontrinoandassociates.com

What this company offers: *We have been assisting our clients with Behaviorally-Based Interviews for over 20 years in Washington State, Idaho, Oregon, California, Alaska, and Hawaii. We help our clients identify potential interview areas and topics through a straightforward job analysis procedure. We then interview supervisors and employees using a critical-incident interview process. This process involves identifying actual examples of excellent and poor performance. These examples are used to create Behaviorally-Based questions. We provide consulting services in employee selection, performance appraisal, employee surveys, and organization development.*

Selection Resources.com

4090 Westown Parkway #304
West Des Moines, Iowa 50266
Tel.: 515-221-0850
Email: TMH@selectionresources.com
Web site: www.selectionresources.com

What this company offers: *Thirty years in staffing services and professional interviewing primarily in Central Iowa, but we have clients all over the United States. We provide Internet assessment testing and suggest Behaviorally-Based Interview questions as part of the assessment reports.*

Silverwood Associates

P.O. Box 363
Sharon Center, Ohio 44274
Tel.: 330-239-1646
Email: silverasoc@aol.com

What this company offers: *Over a decade of experience designing custom Behavior-Based Interview systems as part of an overall selection strategy for organizations. We conduct workshops and train-the-trainer sessions on selecting and interviewing individuals. The model uses a competency approach, which can be linked to other systems such as hiring, development, performance appraisal, and succession planning.*

Skill Masters Training, Inc.

3013 S. Wolf Road, #294
Westchester, IL 60154
Tel.: 708-449-0122
Email: john@skillmasters.com
Web site: www.skillmasters.com

What this company offers: *We deliver a one-day workshop in the United States and Canada entitled Behavioral Interviewing. The audience for this seminar includes supervisors, managers, and line employees who interview job applicants. The workshop teaches participants how to conduct a Behavioral Interview and also reviews the entire hiring process from job vacancy to the new employee's first day on the job.*

TD Madison and Associates

4108 Holly Road
Virginia Beach, Virginia 23451
Tel.: 757-425-9950
Email: dmadison@tdmadison.com
Web site: www.tdmadison.com

What this company offers: *TD Madison and Associates is a national retained Executive Search and Assessment company. Behavioral-Based Interviewing has been the foundation of candidate assessment used by TD Madison and Associates for the past two decades. TD Madison has also authored the "Art of Hiring," a behavioral-based approach to interviewing.*

Technical Interviews

7512 N.W. 82nd Street
Kansas City, Missouri 64152
Tel.: 816-741-7695
Email: admin@technicalinterviews.com
Web site: www.technicalinterviews.com

What this company offers: *We provide technical skills testing and technical interviewing guides globally to qualify a candidate or prepare for the technical interview. This presentation covers what you need to train your interviewers in preparing for the interview, the importance of developing competencies, Behavioral-Based Interviewing techniques, and legal issues of which you must be aware.*

ToThePoint Consulting

1108 Farrington Drive
Knoxville, TN 37923
Tel.: 865-659-6411
Email: marcymeldahl@comcast.net

What this company offers: *We work with client companies in east and middle Tennessee and northwest Georgia to understand the position's duties;*

the ideal candidate's knowledge, skills, and abilities; and, if possible, information about the position's supervisor and the company's culture. From that we craft insightful questions. We help the client learn to listen not only to the candidate's answers, but to "listen between the lines" as well.

Training Dynamics
175 Main Street, Suite 506
White Plains, NY 10601
Tel.: 914-948-8065
Email: td@trainingdynamicsweb.com
Web site: www.trainingdynamicsweb.com

What this company offers: *Training Dynamics' program, "Dynamic Interviewing: Hiring Right the First Time," teaches anyone who conducts employment interviews how to improve their effectiveness in selection. The program, available in both generic and customized versions, includes modules on Planning the Interview, Conducting the Interview, and Evaluating the Applicant. Training Dynamics provides related consulting assistance in the areas of competency model development, creation of interview guides and/or competency-based interview questions, and the design of effective selection processes.*

Working Resources
P.O. Box 471525
San Francisco, CA 94147-1525
Tel.: 415-546-1252
Email: mbrusman@workingresources.com
Web site: www.workingresources.com

What this company offers: *How to Assess, Select, Coach and Retain Emotionally Intelligent People—This workshop provides effective techniques to increase your ability to attract, select, coach, and keep top people critical for a company's success. If you want to build a resilient and fast company where people love to work, you have to know how to hire and keep great talent. The combination of Behavior-Based Interviewing and psychological testing for employment screening can help better predict a candidate's success on the job. Services the San Francisco Bay Area and beyond.*

The Authors as Resources

Combined, we have more than 30 years' experience as careers-industry practitioners as well as extensive experience in corporate environments. Both of us are seasoned presenters to corporate, peer, and job-seeker audiences, and we are available to speak to your organization on a variety of topics, such as

- Behavior-Based Interviewing
- Total Hiring Process in Candidate Selection
- Résumé-Mining: Finding Information Gems
- Why Good Employees Leave
- Inside Secrets of Interview Preparation: How to Recognize and Work Around Practiced Responses
- Talent and Leadership Development
- Build High-Performance Teams
- How to Motivate and Retain Employees

Please contact either of us for more information:

Lori Davila—www.loridavila.com—Tel. 678-637-2837
    —Email lori@atlantacareermarketing.com
Louise Kursmark—Best Impression Career Services, Inc.
    —www.yourbestimpression.com—Tel. 888-792-0030
    —Email LK@yourbestimpression.com

Forms Library

Job Description Worksheet

JOB SPECIFICS

Position Title: _____

Reports To: _____

Supervises: _____

Division/Department: _____

Location: _____

Salary Grade: _____

Employment Status: _____

Travel: _____

Date: _____

POSITION PURPOSE

(What is the overall purpose of this position? Why does it exist?)

_____

_____

_____

_____

DUTIES AND RESPONSIBILITIES

(List the major job responsibilities in order of importance.)

1. _____

_____

2. _____

_____

3. _____

_____

4. _____

_____

5. _____

_____

6. _____

_____

7. _____

_____

Job Description Worksheet—Page 2

QUALIFICATIONS

(List minimum requirements in education background, specialized knowledge, experience and skills needed, and certifications.)

1. _____
   _____

2. _____
   _____

3. _____
   _____

4. _____
   _____

5. _____
   _____

6. _____
   _____

7. _____
   _____

OTHER KEY ITEMS TO CONSIDER

(Physical job requirements, who this employee will be communicating with, or measurable performance standards, for example. Are there any future plans that should be taken into consideration?)

1. _____
   _____

2. _____
   _____

3. _____
   _____

4. _____
   _____

5. _____
   _____

6. _____
   _____

7. _____
   _____

Job Competency Chart

Competency Category	Competency Name	Top Performance Actions/ Proficiency Required
SKILLS		
Technical Knowledge and Skills		
Behaviors (performance skills)		
MOTIVATIONS		
Job Fit		
Company Fit		

The Interview Guide

Position _____   **Interviewer Name** _____

Candidate Name _____   **Date** _____

POSITION SUMMARY

Position Reports To: _____   Position Supervises: _____

Division/Dept: _____   Location: _____

Duties and Responsibilities:

Qualifications:

Measurable Performance Standards/Goals:

COMPETENCY SUMMARY

COMPETENCIES	INTERVIEWERS ASSIGNED			
List interviewers at right and check-mark when assigning a specific competency. Use at least two interviewers for each competency.				
1.				
2.				
3.				
4.				
5.				
6.				
7.				
8.				
9.				
10.				
11.				
12.				

The Interview Guide (*continued*)

TECHNICAL KNOWLEDGE AND SKILLS COMPETENCIES

Technical Knowledge and Skills Competency: _____

Top Performance Action(s)/Proficiency Required: _____

_____

Questions	**Responses**
1.	Situation _____
	_____
	Actions _____
	_____
	_____
Satisfied / Dissatisfied?	_____
_____	_____
_____	Results _____
_____	_____
_____	_____

2.	Situation _____
	_____
	Actions _____
	_____
	_____
Satisfied / Dissatisfied?	_____
_____	_____
_____	Results _____
_____	_____
_____	_____

3.	Situation _____
	_____
	Actions _____
	_____
	_____
Satisfied / Dissatisfied?	_____
_____	_____
_____	Results _____
_____	_____
_____	_____

The Interview Guide (*continued*)

PERFORMANCE SKILLS (BEHAVIORS) COMPETENCIES

Performance Skills (Behaviors) Competency: _____

Top Performance Action(s) Required: _____

_____

_____

Questions	Responses
1.	Situation _____
	_____
	Actions _____
	_____
	_____
Satisfied / Dissatisfied?	_____
_____	Results _____
_____	_____
_____	_____
2.	Situation _____
	_____
	Actions _____
	_____
	_____
Satisfied / Dissatisfied?	_____
_____	Results _____
_____	_____
_____	_____
3.	Situation _____
	_____
	Actions _____
	_____
	_____
Satisfied / Dissatisfied?	_____
_____	Results _____
_____	_____
_____	_____

The Interview Guide (*continued*)

CANDIDATE MOTIVATIONS	
Questions	**Responses**
1.	Situation _____
	Actions _____
Satisfied / Dissatisfied?	
_____	
_____	Results _____
_____	
2.	Situation _____
	Actions _____
Satisfied / Dissatisfied?	
_____	
_____	Results _____
_____	
3.	Situation _____
	Actions _____
Satisfied / Dissatisfied?	
_____	
_____	Results _____
_____	

List candidate motivators identified as a result of questioning:

_____

_____

_____

The Interview Guide (*continued*)

JOB-FIT COMPETENCY MOTIVATIONS

Job Fit Competency: _____

Top Performance Action(s): _____

_____

_____

Questions	**Responses**
1.	Situation _____
	_____
	Actions _____
	_____
	_____
Satisfied / Dissatisfied?	_____
_____	Results _____
_____	_____
_____	_____
2.	Situation _____
	_____
	Actions _____
	_____
	_____
Satisfied / Dissatisfied?	_____
_____	Results _____
_____	_____
_____	_____
3.	Situation _____
	_____
	Actions _____
	_____
	_____
Satisfied / Dissatisfied?	_____
_____	Results _____
_____	_____
_____	_____

The Interview Guide (*continued*)

COMPANY-FIT COMPETENCY MOTIVATIONS

Company Fit Competency: _____

Top Performance Action(s): _____

_____

_____

Questions	Responses
1.	Situation _____
	_____
	Actions _____
	_____
	_____
Satisfied / Dissatisfied?	_____
_____	Results _____
_____	_____
_____	_____

2.	Situation _____
	_____
	Actions _____
	_____
	_____
Satisfied / Dissatisfied?	_____
_____	Results _____
_____	_____
_____	_____

3.	Situation _____
	_____
	Actions _____
	_____
	_____
Satisfied / Dissatisfied?	_____
_____	Results _____
_____	_____
_____	_____

The Interview Guide (*continued*)

OTHER PREPARED INTERVIEW QUESTIONS

Question 1: _____

_____

    Answer: _____

    _____

    _____

    _____

Question 2: _____

_____

    Answer: _____

    _____

    _____

    _____

Question 3: _____

_____

    Answer: _____

    _____

    _____

    _____

Question 4: _____

_____

    Answer: _____

    _____

    _____

    _____

The Interview Guide (*continued*)

SUMMARY OF INTERVIEW QUESTIONS

Competency Name: _____

Top Performance Action(s): _____

_____

_____

Interviewer #1 Name _____

    Question 1 _____

    _____

    Question 2 _____

    _____

    Question 3 _____

    _____

Interviewer #2 Name _____

    Question 1 _____

    _____

    Question 2 _____

    _____

    Question 3 _____

    _____

Interviewer #3 Name _____

    Question 1 _____

    _____

    Question 2 _____

    _____

    Question 3 _____

    _____

The Interview Guide (*continued*)

RATING SHEET

Candidate's Name: _____

Position: _____

Rate each competency on a scale from 1 to 3 by circling the rating.

3 = Very Strong Evidence of Desired Competency (Provided several specific and complete examples)

2 = Some Evidence of Desired Competency (Provided only one specific and complete example)

1 = No Evidence of Desired Competency (Could not provide any specific examples or provided incomplete or vague examples)

Competency Name	Rating		
_____	1	2	3
_____	1	2	3
_____	1	2	3
_____	1	2	3
_____	1	2	3
_____	1	2	3
_____	1	2	3
_____	1	2	3
_____	1	2	3
_____	1	2	3
_____	1	2	3
_____	1	2	3

List candidate motivators identified as a result of questioning:

_____

_____

_____

_____

The Interview Guide (*continued*)

RATING SUMMARY SHEET

Candidate's Name: _____

Position: _____

Rate each competency on a scale from 1 to 3 by circling the rating.

3 = Very Strong Evidence of Desired Competency (Provided several specific and complete examples)

2 = Some Evidence of Desired Competency (Provided only one specific and complete example)

1 = No Evidence of Desired Competency (Could not provide any specific examples or provided incomplete or vague examples)

Record each interviewer's rating for each competency.

	Summary of Ratings		
	Interviewer Name	Interviewer Name	Interviewer Name
Competency Name	Rating	Rating	Rating
_____	_____	_____	_____
_____	_____	_____	_____
_____	_____	_____	_____
_____	_____	_____	_____
_____	_____	_____	_____
_____	_____	_____	_____
_____	_____	_____	_____
_____	_____	_____	_____
_____	_____	_____	_____
_____	_____	_____	_____
_____	_____	_____	_____
_____	_____	_____	_____

List candidate motivators identified as a result of questioning:

_____

_____

_____

_____

Index

About the Authors

Lori Davila is a nationally recognized career coach, professional networker, speaker, and writer who specializes in developing individuals, teams, leaders, and organizations to achieve peak performance. She writes a professional development and networking column for the *Atlanta Journal-Constitution* and regularly contributes to the *Wall Street Journal*. Lori specializes in corporate career management and outplacement, hiring and selection, assessments, marketing, resume writing, and in identifying opportunities through networking. She also helps individuals create marketing strategies to achieve their career goals . . . fast. Lori lives in Atlanta, Georgia, with her husband, Mike.

Louise Kursmark is professionally certified as a master resume writer, interview trainer, and job-search coach. She has earned six national awards for excellence in resume writing and is the author of 12 books on career topics such as resumes, cover letters, and career planning. In addition to working one-on-one with executive clients worldwide, she is a frequent speaker and presenter to both industry and general audiences. A native New Englander, she currently resides in Cincinnati with her husband, son, and daughter.